Creativity in the Communicative Arts

Creativity in the Communicative Arts:

A Selective Bibliography

1960–1970

edited by

Marvin E. Ceynar

compiled by

Dorothy Jorstad   Lorene Linder

Donald Phillips   Jean Porter

The Whitston Publishing Company
Troy, New York
1975

PREFACE

The original idea for this bibliography had its inception during a course which I initiated and coordinated entitled, "Creativity in the Communicative Arts," at Northern Illinois University in Dekalb, Illinois, February 3 through May 26, 1970. This series of fifteen evening seminars was designed to explore the latest innovations in the communications field.

There are many publications on the subject of creativity, but there is no known bibliography on the topic of creativity in the communicative arts. After consulting with four N.I.U. librarians--Dorothy Jorstad (now at Kishwaukee College Library in Malta, Illinois), Lorene Linder, Donald Phillips (now at the University of Illinois), and Jean Porter--in the summer of 1970, we decided to begin such a bibliography. It soon became apparent that a selective bibliography carefully done would be more valuable than a massive comprehensive work that fewer persons might consult; also, the man-hours spent on this shorter book of 1256 titles (not counting several duplications) turned out to be some three years, off and on--a longer work would mean a prohibitive amount of time.

Generally, each librarian did research in the area of his or her speciality. Consequently, Dorothy Jorstad covered the areas of advertising, film, mass media (radio, TV, and journalism), education, and group communication (philosophy and psychology). Lorene Linder did the sections on art, assisted with poetry (periodicals), and helped edit individual entries to avoid unnecessary duplication. Donald Phillips researched the subject of music. Jean Porter handled the topics of fiction, speech, and theatre, and assisted with poetry (books). Hence, we have produced an interdisciplinary research tool.

We have limited the bibliography primarily to the years 1960-1970, with occasional references to prior and subsequent years. We also limited the research to the area of communication. For instance, dance, although being an expressive art, was not included. The more traditional communication fields were our primary concern. As for the word "creativity" it typically signified innovations of a valuable sort. In addition, we emphasized articles more than books, theses, or dissertations, because a compilation of these is more difficult to obtain than the comparatively few scholarly works on the subject under discussion. Most of the research is in English because our intended audience mainly includes practitioners, professors, and any educated adults who are interested in creativity in communication from the viewpoints of a specialist in a communication area or of a generalist. Further elaboration on the approximate perimeters of the bibliography is stated at the beginning of each of the nine bibliographical sections.

Although care has been taken to use the best bibliographical indexes in doing our research, we have obtained the advice of professional leaders from Northern Illinois University who are recognized for their competence within their fields. The following professors from nine departments gave invaluable suggestions:

Art--Jack Arends, Charles Cannon, and Alice Holcomb
Communication Services--Clair R. Tettemer
Education--K. R. Getschman
English--Glenn Meeter and Russell F. Durning
Marketing--Daniel K. Stewart
Music--Stanley S. Ballinger, Alice Berning, and Eleanor Tipton
Psychology--Martin F. Kaplan
Speech Communication--Halbert E. Gulley
Theatre Arts--Richard L. Arnold and Dennis Rich

Among other persons consulted were T. Jan Wiseman of Kishwaukee College, and Mortimer J. Adler, Director of the Institute for Philosophical Research, San Francisco, California.

The individuals above have saved us from committing many

errors. But, for what is printed here, we are solely responsible.

More information, however, needs to be shared on the criteria for inclusion of materials in this bibliography. Our primary concern was not to be exhaustive but to probe thoughtfully the interdisciplinary nature of creativity in the communicative arts and to spur further reading and research in this kind of creativity.

Specific concerns, at times very unique, were expressed by the librarians in each of the eleven sections. It is helpful, therefore, to summarize their individual standards for their bibliographical citations.

Under "Advertising," BUSINESS PERIODICALS INDEX, PUBLIC AFFAIRS INFORMATION AFFAIRS SERVICE, APPLIED SCIENCE AND TECHNOLOGY INDEX, and some general indexing services covering the years since 1960 were used to compile the citations. The citations are intended to start the general reader or worker in the field in the direction of creativity. This person, hopefully, will become much more aware of the interdisciplinary ramifications of advertising.

Advertising is meant to catch the eye and the ear. Some advertisements can communicate favorably to all persons, if it is possible to be creative in the same way to all persons. The advertising business has one of the greatest potentials to be creative because it is a "selling" field. To get the buyer's interest can bring out true creativity. Just being different or new is not being creative. Finding that elusive quality that is true creativity is a must in the advertising business. Examples of imaginative and unimaginative creativity and of just plain "different" ideas are presented to show how elusive this creativity business is.

With few exceptions, the books and articles listed in the "Art" section were written in English and published in the last decade. The requirements for inclusion were that the writer either discuss communication in art or in some sense assume that art does communicate and that he also deal with some aspect of creativity in one or more of the fine arts, such as sculpture, painting, or architecture.

The level of sophistication ranges from texts which can be read easily by any educated adult to scholarly materials of value to specialists in psychology, art, sociology, or philosophy. The bibliography is not intended to be exhaustive but does seek to draw together from the literature of several disciplines representative treatments of the subject.

Education is one of the major "industries" in the United States today. With the mass media, films, art, music, literature, and drama all being part of both formal and informal education, there should be no limit to how creative it can be. Moreover, education as a field is communication. Education must compete especially with the mass media and recreation for time; hence, creativity is vital. This bibliography could be a start in thinking creativity.

This bibliography will be of most use to the general reader or the person starting research in the field. Elementary and secondary school teachers may find it interesting and helpful in searching for ways to present their subjects. There was no formal rationale set up for inclusion--articles and books were chosen as examples of what is creative in education. An attempt was made to include some well-known authors and authorities in education.

The indexing services used most were EDUCATION INDEX and PUBLIC AFFAIRS INFORMATION SERVICE. Other specialized indexing and abstraction services can be used depending on the facet of education one is interested in, for instance, BUSINESS EDUCATION INDEX.

The fiction bibliography includes books and articles published from 1960-1970 which deal primarily with creativity in the fiction of that decade. Much literary criticism was published during this period, but only material concerned specifically with literature's creative aspects is included in this listing.

While this is not an exhaustive list, it is intended to be representative. Material on all genres of modern American fiction--novel, short story, science fiction, black fiction, etc.--is included. Books and articles about specific authors were not included unless they also dealt with, in some degree, creativity in modern fiction. Since this bibliography is intended for use in both secondary schools and colleges and universities, the reading level of the books and articles comprising this list ranges from popular to scholarly. Sources consulted for materials dealing with fiction and creativity or the communicative aspects of fiction included the PMLA bibliographies, the LIBRARY OF CONGRESS CATALOG: BOOKS: SUBJECTS, READERS' GUIDE, and SOCIAL SCIENCES AND HUMANITIES INDEX.

The decade of the 60's is the basic time span used in making up the film citations. They will be useful mainly to the general reader or the person beginning to feel his way into the film making industry. Films are made to communicate ideas and feelings. The problem, therefore, becomes one of injecting creativity into these productions. Films are also made to communicate in almost all disciplines and are essentially interdisciplinary.

Listings were included on a basis of trying to show this interdisciplinary function as well as to try to define film creativity. The citations were selected from the major indexing services using the appropriate subject headings. They were limited in number because there was no intention of producing an exhaustive or definitive bibliography. Hopefully, the persons using this bibliography will come up with a sound definition and understanding of creativity in films.

For the most part, group communication citations were taken from standard indexing services covering 1960-1970. In a very few instances, earlier or later items were included to suggest beginnings of creativity in a field or to show continuity into the 70's. The listings chosen will bring out various facets of creativity. They are a very small number compared to the abundance of articles that can be found by searching through the general and specific indexing and abstracting services in the various disciplines.

This bibliography will probably be of most use to the nonspecialist or to the person who is beginning research in college courses involving the various communicative disciplines. Thus, it may appeal to the one who is only curious or new in the field rather than to the person well into advanced study or already teaching theories of creativity.

There were no special requirements for inclusion in this section since it can be viewed as the beginning of our entire bibliography on creativity. Entries are meant to be only a beginning for and examples of creativity in the various forms of communication.

Radio, television, and journalism have all been included in the category of "Mass Media," since these three areas overlap in many aspects. Again, the general indexing services were used and no hard lines were drawn as to what to include. These disciplines are essentially communication. An attempt was made to include citations that are designed to arouse curiosity and imagination rather than to be too overly precise as to creativity, PER SE. The bibliography will be more useful to the general reader, student, or media worker than to the theorist.

The mass media deal with promotion, advertising, news events, education, special reports, entertainment, and unusual programs. If these media do not try to be creative, then the communication is only repetitious and boring. This bibliography which takes items from the 1960's, will light the way for those searching for creativity in the mass media. It is not nor could it hardly be comprehensive. Real creativity can be measured only by the reaction it sparks in those exposed to the media. What seems creative to one person--what lights his spark--may be boring to another.

The music bibliography covers a ten year period from 1960-1970. Its academic scope is limited primarily to education needs on the secondary school level, to music research, and to composition at the university or college level.

Books on music include titles about measurement of ability and recognition of academically talented students in music, exploration of modern music, composition in jazz, and electronic and other media. Periodical items attempt to lead the reader to more timely materials which include aleatoric music, psychoacoustics, computer-assisted teaching, and the synthesizer as well as considerations of creativity.

For purposes of the "Poetry" section, the word POETRY is understood to encompass forms of rhythmic expression ranging from spontaneous folk utterances to the most abstruse and sensitive development of poetic art.

Requirements for inclusion are that the author of the book or article discuss either the creative process itself in the writing of poetry or the poem as a medium of communication.

The poetry bibliography is far from exhaustive. The main indexes used in the search were the SOCIAL SCIENCES AND HUMANITIES INDEX, PSYCHOLOGICAL ABSTRACTS, BRITISH HUMANITIES INDEX, BIBLIOGRAPHIC INDEX, SOCIOLOGICAL ABSTRACTS, EDUCATICN INDEX, and the READERS' GUIDE. In addition, the LIBRARY OF CONGRESS CATALOG: BOOKS: SUBJECTS and the PMLA bibliographies were searched for books dealing specifically with either the creative process or with poetry as a means of communication. The search resulted in the drawing together of materials from several disciplines into a list designed to serve the needs of teachers and of general readers interested in the creative process and in poetry as a communicative art.

Because little was written about the creative aspects of speech communication until the latter half of the 1960's, most of the entries are dated 1965 or later. Books, dissertations, and periodical articles are included in this bibliography. The content of these materials ranges from popular to scholarly, making this bibliography useful for college and university faculty members as well as high school students.

The LIBRARY OF CONGRESS CATALOG: BOOKS: SUBJECTS, DISSERTATION ABSTRACTS, the "Bibliography of Rhetoric and Public Address" in SPEECH MONOGRAPHS, Matlon's INDEX TO JOURNALS IN SPEECH COMMUNICATION THROUGH 1969, and the READERS' GUIDE were among the sources consulted.

Although not an exhaustive list, the "Theatre" section endeavors to provide, for use by high school and college students and teachers, a representative selection of books, dissertations, and periodical articles written during the 1960's on creative aspects of and trends in contemporary American theatre.

An attempt was made to include material about all the major new forms of theatrical expression. Among sources consulted for information were: LIBRARY OF CONGRESS CATALOG: BOOKS:

SUBJECTS, Fredric M. Litto's AMERICAN DISSERTATIONS ON THE DRAMA AND THE THEATRE: A BIBLIOGRAPHY, the PMLA bibliographies, GUIDE TO THE PERFORMING ARTS, and READERS' GUIDE.

Here, then, are the eleven topics as they were approached by the four librarians and me. Not all the indexes we used are listed, but they, generally, are standard university library reference tools. Again, what we hope to have accomplished is to have provided a convenient and stimulating interdisciplinary source of information for those interested in studying creativity in the communication arts.

Marvin Ceynar
Dorothy Jorstad
Lorene Linder
Donald Phillips
Jean Porter

DeKalb, Illinois
May 23, 1973

TABLE OF CONTENTS

CREATIVITY IN ADVERTISING

PERIODICALS

"Ad Men Pick the Winners (and Get Spanked for Some Losers)."
RAILWAY AGE 164:16-18, May 20, 1968.

"Adfolk at AA Creative Workshop Will Analyze Many Winning Ads."
ADVERTISING AGE 40:18, May 12, 1969.

"Advertisers Turn to That Old Black Magic to Spur Sales, Traub
Reports." ADVERTISING AGE 38:20, August 7, 1967.

"Annual Advertising Age Creative Workshop; 12th. Chicago."
ADVERTISING AGE 40:1, August 4, 1967.

"Art Director of Year Honor Comes to Massey After Decade With
Great Ideas." ADVERTISING AGE 38:10, June 26, 1967.

"Avis Contest Asks for Bugs that Bug Secretaries." ADVERTISING
AGE 39:8, April 15, 1968.

Barton, R. "Rich Language of Advertising." MEDIA-SCOPE
11:81, November, 1967.

Berry, S. N. "Creative Role: to Copywrite or Copycat?" SPONSOR
18:61, October 5, 1964.

"Breaking Through the Ivy Curtain." SPONSOR 21:50-52, September, 1967.

Bressler, H. "How to Write Ads That Sell--Award Juries."
PRINTERS INK 294:64, May 12, 1967.

Buszak, B. "In Outdoor, a Growth Medium With New Standards: Rotating Painted Bulletins." MEDIA-SCOPE 11:95-96, June, 1967.

Calkins, E. E. "My Creativity Philosophy--As It Grew Over Half a Century." PRINTERS INK 295:28, September 8, 1967.

"Close Creative-Research Gap, Panelists Urge ANA Seminar." ADVERTISING AGE 39:24, March 4, 1968.

"Consumer, Industrial Ad Creativity to Be Presented, Discussed At Workshop." ADVERTISING AGE 40:86, May 26, 1969.

"Creativity; Special Report." PRINTERS INK 276:31-78, September 15, 1961.

Daniels. "Plenty of Advertising Uncreativity Is Masquerading As Creativity." ADVERTISING AGE 39:2, November 4, 1968.

"Dealer Displays Use Lights, Motion in Space and Time." ADVERTISING AGE 38:52, December 11, 1967.

"Deodorizing Commercial TV; Public Sick of Soap and Fraud." TIMES EDUCATIONAL SUPPLEMENT 2373:636, November 11, 1960.

"Dichter Favors Psychedelic Ideas." ADVERTISING AGE 38:34, October 16, 1967.

"Do's Don'ts of Many Kinds of Ads Outlined by Workshop Speakers." ADVERTISING AGE 40:3, August 11, 1969.

Eschenfelder, A. H. "Creating an Environment For Creativity." RESEARCH MANAGEMENT 11:231-240, July, 1968.

Field, P. L. "Marketing Creativity under Fire." BUSINESS MANAGEMENT 36:18-21, June, 1969.

Fitz-Gibbon, B. "Mac's Gimbels & Me." (Review of Book--by

Advertising

J. Walker, Jr.) EDITOR & PUBLISHER 100:62, June 10, 1967.

Fox, J. J. "It's True, Charlie--and You Better Believe It!" SALES
MANAGEMENT 100:122-124, January 15, 1968.

Friedman, L. "Creative Life Calls Priest to New Work." ADVER-
TISING AGE 38:38, January 15, 1968.

Getchell, J. S. "Creative Credo of Stirling Getchell: The Speech
That He Never Made; Ads of the 30's Teach Admen Some
Lessons for the 60's." ADVERTISING AGE 39:67-68, March
18, 1968.

Gossage, H. L. "Quit Kidding Public; Please It, Instead, and
Avoid Overstatement; How to be Creative About Next to
Nothing." ADVERTISING AGE 32:90, October 29, 1962.

"Great Sartorial Reformation." MARKETING/COMMUNICATIONS
295:39-41, November, 1967.

Hall, W. B. "Personality Inventory Correlates of Creativity
Among Architects." JOURNAL OF APPLIED PSYCHOLOGY
53:322-326, August, 1969.

Heekin, J. R., Jr. "How I Would Get More Creativity from My
Agency." ADVERTISING AGE 39:21-23, December 23, 1968.

"Industrial Ads Desert Dullsville." SALES MANAGEMENT 102:88,
May 1, 1969.

"International Advertising Has a New Baby (Worldwide Creative
Director)." INTERNATIONAL ADVERTISER 10,1:14-15,
1969.

Jones, K. "Advertising: Greatest Opportunity for Creativity."
ADVERTISING AGE 39:100, September 9, 1968.

Jones, Kensinger. "The Executive Reel." JOURNAL OF
ADVERTISING 1,1: In Press, 1972.

Joyce, W. "Care and Feeding of the Idea Creative Process."
PRINTERS INK 283:105-108, June 14, 1963.

Karl, S. "Creative Man Helmut Krone Talks About the Making of
an Ad." ADVERTISING AGE 39:107-108, October 14, 1968.

"Kudos for an Adman of the Year Runner-up; and a Few Kind
Words for Some Others." INDUSTRIAL MARKETING 53:61-64,
February, 1968.

LaRue, S. M. "Paintings That Talk Back!" ARTS & ACTIVITIES
63:28-31, May, 1968.

Lorimer, E. S. and S. W. Dunn. "Four Measures of Cross-cultural
Effectiveness." JOURNAL OF ADVERTISING RESEARCH
7:11-13, December, 1967.

McCabe, E. A. "Understanding Creativity." SPONSOR 19:66-67,
May 31, 1965.

McDermid, C. D. "Some Correlates of Creativity in Engineering
Personnel" (bibliography). JOURNAL OF APPLIED RESEARCH
49:14-19, February, 1965.

McMahan, H. W. "Ratio to Sell to TV Creativity Is Crucial."
ADVERTISING AGE 40:33, July 28, 1969.

---. "Warns Against Misguided Creativity. (TV Commercials)."
SPONSOR 19:25, April 19, 1965.

Margulies, W. P. "Can a Package Help Create a Great Ad Cam-
paign?" ADVERTISING AGE 39:49-50, April 15, 1968.

Maynard, H. E. "General Semantics; Idea Organizer." PRINTERS
INK 277:48-50, October 13, 1961.

Mee, J. F. "Ideational Items--a Collection." BUSINESS HORIZONS
12:53-60, June, 1969.

Advertising

Meyer, C. "How Big Agencies Are Countering the Surge of the Smalls with Creativity." TELEVISION 25:28-29, May, 1968.

Moss, J. J. "What Is Creativity in Industrial Arts..." JOURNAL OF INDUSTRIAL ARTS EDUCATION 24:24-27, January, 1965.

Nelson, R. C. "Harper's Happy Hippies." MARKETING/COMMUNI-CATIONS 295:50-52, October, 1967.

"New Advertising Art of One-liners and Sight Gags." MARKETING/ COMMUNICATIONS 297:50-51, May, 1969.

Novak, G. "Role of Creativity in Marketing." PRINTERS INK 281:26-27, December 21, 1962.

"Noxell Contest Appeals to Lyric Writers 12 to 20." ADVERTISING AGE 38:2, November 13, 1967.

Ochs, M. B. "Games Ad Men Play: Humor." MEDIA -SCOPE 11:123-124, June, 1967.

"Old Taylor Drive Aimed At Negro Market Honors Little Known Ingenious American." ADVERTISING AGE 38:12, December 11, 1967.

"Papers Hail Originality in Progress Edition Ads." (Honolulu Advertiser & Star-Bulletin). EDITOR AND PUBLISHER 101:24, March 23, 1968.

Polykoff, S. "Think It Out Square, Then Say It with a Flair." BROADCASTING 73:48, December 4, 1967.

Prange, J. "There's More to Art Than Meets the Eye." ARTS & ACTIVITIES 61:6-10, March, 1967.

"Racing Car Exhibit Boosts Sales by $1,800 and Traffic by 2,000." Key Rexall Drug, Rockford, Illinois. AMERICAN DRUGGIST 156:66, July 3, 1967.

Raleigh, H. P. "Creativity, Intelligence, and Art Education" (bibliography). ART EDUCATION 19:14-17, November, 1966.

"Rules Can Jive with Creative Effort, Politz Tells Marketers." ADVERTISING AGE 39:3, April 29, 1968.

"Safety Oriented Limericks Brighten Mobilift Truck Ads." ADVERTISING AGE 39:100, April 1, 1968.

Schmid, L. "Teaching Art on Television; Austin-San Antolio Area." EDUCATION DIGEST 29:30-31, December, 1963.

Spector, J. J. "Conversation: Paula Green On the Doyle Dane Way." MARKETING /COMMUNICATIONS 297:38-40, May, 1969.

Tannenbaum, S. "Take a Creative Man Out to Lunch." MEDIA-SCOPE 13:87, January, 1969.

"There's Nothing Small About Ad Statuary--Created by Internal Fiberglass." ADVERTISING AGE 38:64, November 27, 1967.

Tinker, J. "How Creativity Gets Through to People: Portfolio of Paintings." PRINTERS INK 269:60, November 13, 1959.

Toensmeier, P. A. "Storage Cartridge for Shipper-Display (Data Sheet)." PAPERBOARD PACKAGING 53:57-58, March, 1968.

Tomkinson, E. G. "Critical Look at Creative Art." GRADE TEACHER 83:56-57, April, 1966.

Tyler, W. "Best Advertising Headlines of 1967." ADVERTISING AGE 38:39-41, December 18, 1967.

---. "Best Campaigns of 1967." ADVERTISING AGE 39:47-48, March 4, 1968.

"Uncle Jackson's Ghost Helps Push Erie's Kochler Beer." ADVERTISING AGE 39:12, April 8, 1968.

Advertising

Weiss, B. "Is Creative Advertising a Young Business?" ADVERTIS-
ING AGE 39:41-42, September 2, 1968.

"What Price Supercreativity?" SALES MANAGEMENT 97:49-51,
118-120, October 15, 1966.

White, Gordon. "Creativity: The X-Factor In Advertising Communication." JOURNAL OF ADVERTISING 1,1: In Press, 1972.

"With Return to Walk a Mile, Camel Revives An Alltime Venerable
Motif." ADVERTISING AGE 38:60, October 2, 1967.

"A Workshop To Feature Blanc On Radio; McMahan. Bellaire On
TV Ads." ADVERTISING AGE 40:28, July 14, 1969.

BOOKS

Cone, Fairfax M. WITH ALL ITS FAULTS: A CANDID ACCOUNT
OF 40 YEARS IN ADVERTISING. Boston: Little, 1969.

Glatzer, Robert. THE NEW ADVERTISING; THE GREAT CAM-
PAIGNS FROM AVIS TO VOLKSWAGEN. 1st. ed. New York:
Citadel Press, 1970.

Noble, Valerie. THE EFFECTIVE ECHO; A DICTIONARY OF
ADVERTISING SLOGANS. New York: Special Libraries
Association, 1970.

Scott, James D., ed. THE CREATIVE PROCESS. Ann Arbor:
Bureau of Business Research, University of Michigan, 1957,
pp. 54-67.

CREATIVITY IN ART

PERIODICALS

"ACLS Inquiry on Creative Arts." ART JOURNAL 21,4:249, Summer, 1962.

Aldrich, Virgil Charles. "Design, Composition, and Symbol." JOURNAL OF AESTHETICS 27,4:379-388, Summer, 1969.

Aler, Jan. "Schooling for Creativity." JOURNAL OF AESTHETICS AND ART CRITICISM 23,1:81-95, Fall, 1964.

Allen, Arthur Henry Burlton. "Art and Life." HIBBERT JOURNAL 56:61-68, October, 1957.

Anand, Mulk Raj. "Hand and the Heart: Notes on the Creative Process in the Folk Imagination." MARG 22:4-10, September, 1969.

Anderson, Jack. "Ferment and Controversy; New Look in Dance and the Arts Keeps Changing Its Sights." DANCE MAGAZINE 43:46-55, August, 1969.

Arnheim, Rudolf. "What Is Art for?" TEACHERS COLLEGE RECORD 66:46-53, October, 1964.

Arragon, Reginald Francis. "History's Changing Image; with Such Permanence As Time Has." AMERICAN SCHOLAR 33:222-233, Spring, 1964.

"Art and Sanity; Case of M. Barnes of East London." NEWSWEEK

73:96-100, May 19, 1969.

"Art in America, Yesterday and Tomorrow" (editorial). ART IN
AMERICA 58:54-55, January-February, 1970.

"Art in the Margin?" TIMES LITERARY SUPPLEMENT 3237:205-
206, March 12, 1964.

Aschenbrenner, Karl. "Creative Receptivity." JOURNAL OF
AESTHETICS 22,2:149-151, Winter, 1963.

Ashton, Dore and Leonard Baskin. "A to B (Originality in Art)."
STUDIO INTERNATIONAL 166:194-197, November, 1963.

Ashton, Dore. "New York Commentary." STUDIO INTERNATIONAL
174:277-279, December, 1967.

---. "Response to Crisis in American Art." ART IN AMERICA
57:24-35, January, 1969.

Bassi, Robert A. "Chicago Aftermath; a Moral Dilemma for Designers." PRINT 22:32-35, November, 1968.

Battcock, Gregory. "Art of the Real, the Development of a Style:
1948-1968." ARTS MAGAZINE 42:44-47, June 1, 1968.

Beardsley, Monroe C. "On the Creation of Art." JOURNAL OF
AESTHETICS AND ART CRITICISM 23,3:291-304, Spring, 1965.

Beloff, John. "Creative Thinking in Art and in Science" (bibliography). BRITISH JOURNAL OF AESTHETICS 10:58-70,
January, 1970.

Berlin, Irving N. "Aspects of Creativity and the Learning Process." AMERICAN IMAGO 17:83-99, Spring, 1960.

Bickford, John H. "What Should I Paint?" AMERICAN ARTIST
32:32-33, 75, October, 1968.

Brien, Alan. "Afterthought (abstract artists seem to be denying that any worthwhile communication can be made)." SPECTATOR 212:609-610, May 1, 1964.

Brittain, W. Lambert and K. R. Beittel. "Analysis of levels of Creative Performance in the Visual Arts." JOURNAL OF AESTHETICS AND ART CRITICISM 19,1:83-90, Fall, 1960.

Brodzky, Anne. "Impermanence." ARTSCANADA 25:4, April, 1968.

Bryson, Lyman. "Training for Creativity." SCHOOL ARTS 60:5-8, September, 1960.

Burton, John. "Creative Philosophy." CALIFORNIA TEACHER'S ASSOCIATION JOURNAL 60:11, January, 1964.

Butor, Michel. "Sources of Contemporary Art." LONDON MAGA- ZINE n.s., 1,4:19-31, July, 1961.

Calas, Nicolas. "Enterprise of Criticism." ART MAGAZINE 42:9, September, 1967.

Cassirer, Thomas. "Africas Olympiad of the Arts: Some Observa- tions on the Dakar Festival." MASSACHUSETTS REVIEW 8:177-184, Winter, 1967.

Castle, Frederick C. "Threat Art: Some Thought on Robert Rauschenberg, Andy Warhol, Elie Faure. 'The Art of the Real,' at the Museum of Modern Art Recent Fads and Other Events." ART NEWS 67:54-55, 65-66, October, 1968.

Clark, Sir Kenneth McKenzie. "Art and Society." CORNHILL MAGAZINE 171:307-325, Fall, 1960.

Clark, Paul Sargent. "Better Living Thru Chemistry?" INDUSTRIAL DESIGN 15:32-37, July, 1968.

Cooper, William. "Mindless Art--an Informal Discussion." TEXAS QUARTERLY 9:64-73, Summer, 1966.

Corkhill, A. A. and R. F. Guenter. "Systematic Approach to Design." ALA JOURNAL 50:75-77, December, 1968.

Cowan, Harvey. "Need for Impermanence." ARTSCANADA 25:6-11, April, 1968.

"Creativity in Architectural Design: the ACSA Committee Reports." AMERICAN INSTITUTE OF ARCHITECTS JOURNAL 42:99-102, September, 1964.

Crowley, C. P. J. "Simultaneous Vision and Human Creativity." CANADIAN ART 17:301-303, September, 1960.

Daemmrich, Horst S. "Friedrich Schiller and Thomas Mann: Parallels in Aesthetics." JOURNAL OF AESTHETICS 24,2:227-249, Winter, 1965.

Davies, Elton M. "Condition of Growth and the Act of Creation." STUDIES IN ART EDUCATION 6:24-33, Spring, 1965.

Davis, Douglas M. "Art and Technology." ART IN AMERICA 56:28-47, January, 1968.

"Devotional Images and Imaginative Devotions: Notes on the Place of Art in Late Medieval Private Piety (with French summary)." GAZETTE DES BEAUX-ARTS 6,73:159-170, March, 1969.

"Dialectic of Modern Art." TIMES p. 11, August 27, 1963.

Drews, Elizabeth Monroe. "Are Intelligence and Talent the Same?" NATIONAL EDUCATION ASSOCIATION JOURNAL 50:40-41, January, 1961.

Ducasse, Curt John. "Art and the Language of the Emotions." JOURNAL OF AESTHETICS AND ART CRITICISM 23,1:109-112, Fall, 1964.

"East Goes West (Avery Brundage Collection)." ECONOMIST

220:819, August 27, 1966.

Ecker, David W. "Artistic Process As Qualitative Problem Solving." JOURNAL OF AESTHETICS AND ART CRITICISM 21,3:283-290, Spring, 1963.

Efron, Arthur. "Technology and the Future of Art." MASSA-CHUSETTS REVIEW 7:677-710, Autumn, 1966.

Ehrenzweiz, Anton. "Art - Anti - Art: Alienation Versus Self-Expression." LISTENER pp. 345-346, 368, February 25, 1960.

Ettlinger, L. D. "German Expressionism and Primitive Art." BURLINGTON MAGAZINE 110:191-201, April, 1968.

Evans, Garth. "Sculpture and Reality." STUDIO INTERNATIONAL 177:61-62, February, 1969.

Feldman, Morton. "Some Elementary Questions: Control of the Material? Or Control of the Experience?" ART NEWS pp. 54-55, April, 1967.

Ferebee, Ann . "Great Graphic Designer of the 20th Century." PRINT 23:23-100, 104, 109, January, 1969.

Fisher, John Lyle. "Art Styles As Cultural Cognitive Maps." AMERICAN ANTHROPOLOGIST 63:79-93, February, 1961.

Fizer, John. "Problem of the Unconscious in the Creative Process As Treated by Soviet Aesthetics." JOURNAL OF AESTHETICS AND ART CRITICISM 21,4:399-406, Summer, 1963.

Frankfurter, Alfred . "Pop Extremities." ART NEWS 63:19, 54-55, September, 1964.

Fry, Roger Eliot. "Double Nature of Painting." APOLLO n.s., 89:363-371, May, 1969.

Fuller, Richard Buckminster. "Design Responsibility."

The Communicative Arts

INDUSTRIAL DESIGN 16:72-75, April, 1969.

Gargano, James William. "Hawthorne's 'The Artist of the Beautiful'." AMERICAN LITERATURE 35:225-230, May, 1963.

Garvin, W. Lawrence. "Creativity and the Design Process."
AMERICAN INSTITUTE OF ARCHITECTS JOURNAL 41:89-90,
June, 1964.

Gavagan, Peter C. "Trends in Modern Art." STUDIO INTERNA-
TIONAL 174:83-84, September, 1967. Reply: D. Thompson,
175:7, January, 1968.

Getzels, J. W. and M. Csikszentmihalzi. "On the Roles, Values
and Performance of Future Artists: a Conceptual and Empirical
Explanation." SOCIOLOGICAL QUARTERLY 9:516-530,
Autumn, 1968.

Gilman, Richard. "Art and History." PARTISAN REVIEW 35:274-286,
Spring, 1968.

Goldin, Amy. "Situation Critical." ART NEWS 67:44-45, 64-67,
March, 1968.

Gombrich, Ernst Hans Josef. "Use of Art for the Study of Sym-
bols." AMERICAN PSYCHOLOGIST 20:34-50, January, 1965.

Gordon, Jan B. "William Morris's Destiny of Art." JOURNAL OF
AESTHETICS AND ART CRITICISM 27,3:271-279, Spring, 1969.

Grossman, Manuel L. "Language of Dada." JOURNAL OF COMMUN-
ICATION 18:4-10, March, 1968.

Hallman, Ralph J. "Aesthetic Motivation in the Creative Arts"
(bibliography). JOURNAL OF AESTHETICS AND ART CRITI-
CISM 23,4:453-459, Summer, 1965.

Hampshire, Stuart. "Conflict Between Art and Politics."
LISTENER 64:629, 635-636, October 13, 1960.

Hanson, Howard. "Artists' Role Today." NEA JOURNAL 50:12-13, January, 1961.

Harrell, Bill J. "Emasculation of Self in Modern Art." CATALYST 3:74-95, Summer, 1967.

Harris, William Henry. "Art Teaching for Creative Thinking." ART JOURNAL 20,2:92-95, Winter, 1960-1961.

Hausman, Carl Ransdell. "Maritain's Interpretation of Creativity in Art." JOURNAL OF AESTHETICS 19,2:215-219, Winter, 1960.

Heckscher, August. "Changing Styles in Art and Entertainment." ANNALS OF THE AMERICAN ACADEMY OF POLITICAL AND SOCIAL SCIENCE 378:109-116, July, 1968.

Henning, Edward B. "Patronage and Style in the Arts: A Suggestion Concerning Their Relations." JOURNAL OF AESTHETICS AND ART CRITICISM 18:464-471, June, 1960.

Henri, Robert. "Duality of the Artist, Relation of the Artist to the Community?" AMERICAN ARTIST 32:5, November, 1968.

Hodin, Josef Paul. "Aesthetics of Modern Art." JOURNAL OF AESTHETICS AND ART CRITICISM 26,2:181-186, Winter, 1967.

---. "Spirit of Modern Art." BRITISH JOURNAL OF AESTHETICS 1:174-184, June, 1961.

Hofstadter, Albert. "Art and Spiritual Validity" (bibliography). JOURNAL OF AESTHETICS AND ART CRITICISM 22,1:9-19, Fall, 1963.

"Inspiration in Art." Special issue. DU; SCHWEIZERISCHE MONATSCHRIFT 20: October, 1960.

"Invention." TIMES LITERARY SUPPLEMENT 3253:561-562, July 2, 1964.

Jacobs, Jay. "Where Do We Come From? What Are We? Where Are We Going? Gauguin's Greatest Painting." HORIZON 11,3: 52-65, Summer, 1969.

Johnson, P. and P. Raven. "James Washington Speaks." ART EDUCATION RECORD 49:286-289, Summer, 1968.

Jones, Peter. "Understanding a Work of Art." BRITISH JOURNAL OF AESTHETICS 9:128-144, April, 1969.

Junker, Howard. "Idea As Art; Anti- object Art." NEWSWEEK 74:81, August 11, 1969.

Kantor, R. E. "Mutability of Art Styles and Research in Perception." ART JOURNAL 27,3:279-283, Spring, 1968.

Karbusicky, Vladimir. "Interaction between Reality-Work of Art - Society." INTERNATIONAL SOCIAL SCIENCE JOURNAL 20,4:644-655, 1968.

Katzumie, Masaru. "Industrial Design in Japan." GRAPHICS 24,138-139:450-458, 474, 1968.

Kauffmann, Stanley. "Can Culture Explode ? Notes on Subsidizing the Arts." COMMENTARY pp. 19-28, August, 1965.

Kavolis, Vytautas Martynas. "Art Content and Economic Reality." AMERICAN JOURNAL OF ECONOMICS AND SOCIOLOGY 24:321-328, July, 1965.

---. "Community Dynamics and Artistic Creativity." AMERICAN SOCIOLOGICAL REVIEW 31:208-217, April, 1966.

---. "Images of the Universe and Styles of Art." INDIAN JOURNAL OF SOCIAL RESEARCH 7:165-172, December, 1966.

---. "Political Determinants of Artist Style." SOCIAL RESEARCH 32:180-192, Summer, 1965.

Art

---. "Political Dynamics and Artistic Creativity." SOCIOLOGY
AND SOCIAL RESEARCH 49:412-424, July, 1965.

---. "Religious Dynamics and Artistic Creativity." INDIAN
SOCIOLOGICAL BULLETIN 4:133-145, January, 1967.

Kay, Jane Holtz. "Artists As Social Reformers." ART IN AMERICA
57:44-47, January, 1969.

Kenner, Hugh. "Art in a Closed Field." VIRGINIA QUARTERLY
REVIEW 38:597-613, Autumn, 1962.

Kermode, Frank. "Tradition and the New Art: Interviews with
Harold Rosenberg and Ernst Gombrich." PARTISAN REVIEW
31:241-252, Spring, 1964.

Koike, Shinji. "Evolution of Industrial Design in Japan As an
Expression of Cultural Values." JOURNAL OF WORLD HISTORY
9,2:380-399, 1965.

Kozloff, Max. "Art." THE NATION 208:347-348, March 17, 1969.

---. "Art and the New York Avant-Garde." PARTISAN REVIEW
31:535-554, Fall, 1964.

---. "Modern Art and the Virtues of Decadence." STUDIO INTER-
NATIONAL 174:189-199, November, 1967.

Kudielka, Robert. "Germany: the New Objectivity." STUDIO
INTERNATIONAL pp. 84-89, February, 1969.

Kuh, Katherine. "Denials, Affirmations and Art." SATURDAY
REVIEW 52:41-42, May 31, 1969.

---. "Inheritor and Activator; Traveling Exhibition of Works by
Moholy - Nagy." SATURDAY REVIEW 52:38-40, July 26, 1969.

---. "What Makes Dutch Art Dutch." SATURDAY REVIEW 52:42-44,
February 1, 1969.

Kuspit, Donald B. "Dewey's Critique of Art for Art's Sake."
JOURNAL OF AESTHETICS AND ART CRITICISM 27,1:93-98,
Fall, 1968. Reply with rejoinder: L. Rothschild, 27,4:461,
Summer, 1969.

Laramee, K. Helena. "Have We Lost Our Marbles?" SCHOOL ARTS
69:36-37, November, 1969.

Levine, Les. "Disposable Transient Environment." ARTSCANADA
25:27-30, April, 1968.

Lichtblau, Charlotte. "Nineteenth Century Hang-ups Today: the
Relevancy of Literary Painting." ARTS 43:44-47, February,
1969.

Lindsay, Sir Harry. "Christian Values and the Arts." HIBBERT
JOURNAL 58:367-371, October, 1959.

Lippold, Richard. "To Make Love to Life." COLLEGE ART
JOURNAL 19:298-306, Summer, 1960.

Loehr, Max. "Some Fundamental Issues in the History of Chinese
Painting." JOURNAL OF ASIAN STUDIES 23:185-193,
February, 1964.

Logsdon, G. "Beholden to No One; Farm People Wyeth Painted."
FARM JOURNAL 93:28-29, 32, 73-74, 101, March, 1969.

Lowry, Wilson McNeil. "University and the Creative Arts." ART
JOURNAL 21,4:233-239, Summer, 1962.

Lubbock, Jules. "First Steps in Contemplation (with French
translation)." MUSEUM (UNESCO) 21,1:60-66, 1968.

Lucie - Smith, Edward. "How Abstract Art Can Influence Thought
and Vision." TIMES p. 11, August 31, 1965.

Lunacharskii, Anatolii Vasilievich. "Philosophical Poems in
Paint and Marble Letters from Italy." SOVIET REVIEW

7:42-56, Summer, 1966.

Lynton, Norbert. "Comment." STUDIO INTERNATIONAL 174:182-183, November, 1967. Reply with rejoinder: Dallwitz, D., 175:64, February, 1968.

Lyons, Joseph. "Paleolithic Aesthetics: the Psychology of Cave Art." JOURNAL OF AESTHETICS AND ART CRITICISM 26,1:107-114, Fall, 1967.

Machamer, Peter K. and George W. Roberts. "Art and Morality." JOURNAL OF AESTHETICS AND ART CRITICISM 26,4:515-519, Summer, 1968.

MacInnes, Colin. "Out of the Way: The Artist-Sociologist." NEW SOCIETY 3:21-22, January, 1963.

MacKinnon, Donald W. "Nature and Nurture of Creative Talent." AMERICAN PSYCHOLOGIST 17:484-495, July, 1962.

Mandel, Oscar. "Artists without Masters." VIRGINIA QUARTERLY REVIEW 39:401-419, Summer, 1963.

Margolis, Joseph. "Creativity, Expression, and Value Once Again." JOURNAL OF AESTHETICS 22,1:21-23, Fall, 1963.

Martland, Thomas R. "Analogy Between Art and Religion." JOURNAL OF PHILOSOPHY 63:509-517, September 29, 1966.

Maslow, Vera. "George Lukacs and the Unconscious." JOURNAL OF AESTHETICS 22,4:465-470, Summer, 1964.

Mathews, Denis and Anna. "Aims of Art in Communist China." GUARDIAN 30: May 18, 1961.

Mathews, Thomas F. "Tillich on Religious Content in Modern Art." ART JOURNAL 27,1:16-19, Fall, 1967.

Melville, Robert. "Under the Bam, under the Boo (John M.

Crawford, Jr. Collection of Chinese Painting and Calligraphy)." NEW STATESMAN AND NATION 70:60, July 9, 1965.

Meredith, William. "Artist as Teacher, the Poet as Trouble-maker." HARVARD EDUCATIONAL REVIEW 36:518-522, Fall, 1966.

Merrill, Francis Ellsworth. "Art and the Self." SOCIOLOGY AND SOCIAL RESEARCH 52:185-194, April, 1968.

Messer, Thomas M. "Impossible Art--Why It Is." ART IN AMERICA 57:30-31, May, 1969.

Metzger, Gustav. "Automata in History." STUDIO INTERNATIONAL 177:107-109, March, 1969.

Miller, Lillian B. "Paintings, Sculpture and the National Character, 1815-1860," JOURNAL OF AMERICAN HISTORY 53:696-707, March, 1967.

Miner, Earl Ray. "Poetic, Picture, Painted Poetry of the Last Instructions to a Painter." MODERN PHILOLOGY 63:288-294, May, 1966.

Mitchell, Donald. "Language of Contemporary Art." LISTENER 63:301-302, February 18, 1960.

Mortellito, Domenico. "Sculpture Overboard! Versatile Urethane for Amphibious Sculpture." INDUSTRIAL DESIGN 15:64-67, January, 1968.

Mothersill, Mary. "Is art a Language (with replies by Vergil C. Aldrich and Vincent Thomas)." JOURNAL OF PHILOSOPHY 62:559-574, October 21, 1965.

Munro, Thomas. "Art and Violence." JOURNAL OF AESTHETICS AND ART CRITICISM 27,3:317-322, Spring, 1969.

Myer, John C. "Need for Rebirth." PSYCHOLOGY 7,1:44-57, 1970.

Nairn, Tom. "New Sensibility." NEW STATESMAN AND NATION 73:408-409, March 24, 1967.

Natanson, Maurice. "Fabric of Expression." REVIEW OF META-PHYSICS 21:491-505, March, 1968.

Negri, Numa Clive. "Art Contra Science--an Inquiry into the Sociological Aspects of the Schism between Science and the Creative Arts." IMPACT OF SCIENCE ON SOCIETY 12,1:61-81, 1962.

Newton, Eric. "Art as Communication." BRITISH JOURNAL OF AESTHETICS 1:71-85, March, 1961.

"No Hanging Space for the Avant Garde." ECONOMIST 222:320, January 28, 1967.

O'Hara, J. D. "Hazlitt and Romantic Criticism of the Fine Arts." JOURNAL OF AESTHETICS AND ART CRITICISM 27,1:73-85, Fall, 1968.

Pelles, Geraldine. "Image of the Artist" (bibliography). JOUR-NAL OF AESTHETICS 21,2:119-137, Winter, 1962.

Pevsner, Nikolaus. "Sources of Art in the Twentieth Century: Exhibition in Paris Organized by the Council of Europe." LISTENER 64:1042-1044, December 8, 1960.

Piene, Otto. "Death Is So Permanent." ARTSCANADA 25:14-17, April, 1968.

Plessner, Helmuth. "Sociological Observati ans on Modern Paint-ing." SOCIAL RESEARCH 29:190-200, Summer, 1962.

Podro, Michael. "Creative Element: Reith Lectures 1960." SPECTATOR 211:178, August 9, 1963.

Portnoy, Julius. "Is the Creative Process Similar in the Arts?" JOURNAL OF AESTHETICS 19,2:191-195, Winter, 1960.

"R. L. Bloore on Permanence." ARTSCANADA 25:31-33,
April, 1968.

Rago, Louise Elliott. "Why People Create." See issues of SCHOOL
ARTS, May 1959 - September 1961.

Raleigh, Henry P. "More on the Creation of Art" (bibliography).
JOURNAL OF AESTHETICS 25,2:159-165, Winter, 1966.

---. "Value and Artistic Alternative: Speculations on Choice in
Modern Art." JOURNAL OF AESTHETICS AND ART CRITICISM
27,3:293-301, Spring, 1969.

Ransohoff, Daniel. "Beauty vs. Blight; Urban Designers and
Social Workers Have Yet to Discover the Benefits of Cooperative
Problem - solving." INDUSTRIAL DESIGN 16:54, March, 1969.

Read, Herbert. "The Necessity of Art." SATURDAY REVIEW
pp. 24-27, December 6, 1969.

"Real, Deep Sparkle." TIMES LITERARY SUPPLEMENT 3279:1181,
December 9, 1964.

Rhodes, James Melvin. "Analysis of Creativity." PHI DELTA
KAPPAN 42:305-310, April, 1961.

Richards, Howard. "Social Responsibility of the Artist." ETHICS
76:221-224, April, 1966.

Robertson, Bryan. "Artist in Our Time." LISTENER 65:1079-
1081, June 22, 1961.

Rosenberg, Bernard and Norris E. Fliegel. "Vanguard Artist in
New York" (reprint). SOCIAL RESEARCH 32:141-162, Summer,
1965.

Rosenberg, Harold. "Art and Work." PARTISAN REVIEW
32:50-56, Winter, 1965.

---. "Art World; B. Newman's Stripe Paintings." NEW YORKER 45:136, 138, 140, 142, April 19, 1969.

---. "Rosenberg on Violence in Art and Other Matters." ART-SCANADA 26:32-33, February, 1969.

Roth, Robert Paul. "Painting as the Communication of Spirit." RELIGION IN LIFE 30:448-457, Summer, 1961.

Rowland, David. "Moral Basis of Design." INDUSTRIAL DESIGN 16:80-81, April, 1969.

Russell, John. "Dubuffet As a Writer." ART IN AMERICA 57:86-89, May, 1969.

---. "Pop Reappraised; Exhibition Hayward Gallery, London." ART IN AMERICA 57:78-89, July, 1969.

Russell, W. M. S. "Art, Science and Man." LISTENER 71:43-45, January 9, 1964; 71:99-101, 113, January 19, 1964.

Sandberg, Willem Jacob Henri Berend. "Creative Use of Leisure." AMERICAN SCHOLAR 35:227-232, Spring, 1966.

Scheick, William Hunt. "Future of the Creative Process." AMERICAN INSTITUTE OF ARCHITECTS JOURNAL 47:41, June, 1967.

Schroeder, Fred E .H. "Andrew Wyeth and the Transcendental Tradition." AMERICAN QUARTERLY 17:559-567, Fall, 1965.

Sechi, Vanina. "Art, Language, Creativity and Kierkegaard." HUMANITAS 5,1:81-97, 1969.

Shahn, Ben. "Artists in Colleges." CHRISTIAN SCHOLAR 43:97-113, Summer, 1960.

Shirey, David L. "Art of Tibet: Exhibition at Asia House, New York." NEWSWEEK 73:91-92, April 28, 1969.

---. "Horror Show; Human Concern/Personal Torment at the Whitney Museum." NEWSWEEK 74:107, November 3, 1969.

---. "Impossible Art; What It Is." ART IN AMERICA 57:32-47, May, 1969.

Sircello, Guy. "Perceptual Acts and Pictorial Art: a Defense of Expression Theory." JOURNAL OF PHILOSOPHY 62:669-677, November 18, 1965.

Sitwell, Sacheverell. "Pleasures of the Senses: Paintings and Drawings of the French Eighteenth Century at the Royal Academy." APOLLO n.s. 87:129-139, February, 1968.

"Sixteen Hundred-year Memory in a Nation's Art." FORTUNE 80:103-109, August 1, 1969.

Smithson, Robert. "Ultramoderne." ARTS MAGAZINE 42:30-32, September, 1967.

Stark, George K. "Silent Images." ART EDUCATION 16:14-19, November, 1963.

Stegeman, Beatrice. "Art of Science." JOURNAL OF AESTHETICS AND ART CRITICISM 27,1:13-19, Fall, 1968.

Strang, Ruth M. "Creative Child." NATIONAL PARENT-TEACHER 54:14-16, February, 1960.

Stuart, Irving R. "Iconography of Group Personality Dynamics: Caricatures and Cartoons." JOURNAL OF SOCIAL PSYCHOLOGY 64:147-156, 1964.

"Super Realism: It's Hard to Tell a Painting from a Photograph." LIFE 66:44-49, June 27, 1969.

Sweeney, James Johnson. "New Directions in Painting." JOURNAL OF AESTHETICS AND ARTS CRITICISM 18:368-377, March, 1960.

Tanaka, Ikko. "Japan's Younger Generation of Designers."
GRAPHICS 24,138-139:332-351, 1968.

Taubes, Frederic. "On the Nature of Artistic Creativity."
AMERICAN ARTIST 23:34, November, 1959.

Taylor, Irving Abraham. "Nature of the Creative Process."
AMERICAN INSTITUTE OF ARCHITECTS JOURNAL 34:48-53,
July, 1960.

Theall, Donald F. "Education of the Senses." CANADIAN ART
pp. 8-10, April, 1966.

Thomas, Vincent. "Kandinsky's Theory of Painting." BRITISH
JOURNAL OF AESTHETICS 9:19-38, January, 1969.

Trego, Charlotte. "Drop City: New Life for Junked Cars."
ARCHITECTURAL FORUM 127:74-75, September, 1967.

Tucker, Eva. "The Painter in the Novel." STUDIO INTERNATION-
AL 174:186-187, November, 1967.

Van Den Hagg, Ernest. "Reflections on Mass Culture." AMERICAN
SCHOLAR 29:227-234, Spring-Summer, 1960. Reply by Gilbert
Seldes 29:450, Summer, 1960.

von Meier, Kurt. "Violence: Art and the American Way!" ART-
SCANADA 25:19-24, 51, April, 1968.

Waley, Hubert D. "Low Level Approaches to Aesthetic Problems."
HIBBERT JOURNAL 59:59-66, October, 1960.

Werner, Alfred. "To Resist the Evil: Art and Tyranny." ARTS
43:40-43, Summer, 1969.

Wiebe, Gerhart David. "Exploration into the Nature of Creativity."
PUBLIC OPINION QUARTERLY 26:389-397, Fall, 1962.

Weiss, Margaret R. "Art for Ad's Sake." SATURDAY REVIEW

52:54-55, June 14, 1969.

Wenkart, Antonia. "Modern Art and Human Development."
AMERICAN JOURNAL OF PSYCHOANALYSIS 20,2:174-179,
1960.

White, S. "Art As A Way of Life." SCHOOL ARTS 64:5-8,
Fall, 1965.

Whitney, Edgar A. "To Know or Not to Know." AMERICAN
ARTIST 32:30-31, September, 1968.

Whyte, Lancelot Law. "Union of Aesthetics and Science."
(with French translation by R. Cahn). MUSEUM (UNESCO)
21,1:8-15, 1968.

Willard, Charlotte. "Violence and Art." ART IN AMERICA 57:36-
43, January, 1969.

Willett, John. "The Arts: the Other Revolution." TIMES LITERARY
SUPPLEMENT 3436:13-14, January 4, 1968.

Williams, Sheldon. "Artists in Outer Space." CONTEMPORARY
REVIEW 209:316-321, December, 1966.

Wilson, Colin Henry. "Can Art Help?" STUDIO 162:86-89, September, 1961.

Wind, Edgar. "Reith Lectures. 1. Art and Anarchy: Our Present
Discontents." LISTENER 64:881-884, November 1, 1960.

Winthrop, Henry. "Technicization of the Aesthetic Impulse--
1. Decadence and Pathology in the Arts." JOURNAL OF HUMAN
RELATIONS 17,1:104-118, 1969.

Wollheim, Richard. "Professor Gombrich." NEW STATESMAN AND
NATION 67:18-19, January 3, 1964.

"World War II Graphics." PRINT 23:24-27, May, 1969.

BOOKS

Anderson, John Mueller. THE REALM OF ART. University Park: Pennsylvania State University Press, 1967.

Anderson, Maxwell. THE BASES OF ARTISTIC CREATION. New Brunswick: Rutgers University Press, 1942.

Arnheim, Rudolf. TOWARD A PSYCHOLOGY OF ART. Berkeley, California: University of California Press, 1966. Review: JOURNAL OF AESTHETICS AND ART CRITICISM (H. Osborne) 26,1:138-141, Fall, 1967.

Art Directors Club of New York. CREATIVITY, AN EXAMINATION OF THE CREATIVE PROCESS: A REPORT ON THE THIRD COMMUNICATIONS CONFERENCE OF THE ART DIRECTORS CLUB OF NEW YORK. Edited by Paul Smith. New York: Hastings House, 1959.

Berdiaev, Nikolai Aleksandrovich. THE MEANING OF THE CREA- TIVE ACT. New York: Harper, 1955.

Brittain, W. Lambert, ed. CREATIVITY AND ART EDUCATION. Washington, D.C.: National Art Education Association, 1964.

Butler, Reginald Cotterell. CREATIVE DEVELOPMENT. New York: Horizon Press, 1963.

Centeno, Augusto, ed. THE INTENT OF THE ARTIST. 1941 Reprint. New York: Russell and Russell, 1970.

Chicago, University of. Committee on Social Thought. THE WORKS OF THE MIND. Chicago: University of Chicago, 1947.

Collier, Graham. FORM, SPACE, AND VISION; DISCOVERING DESIGN THROUGH DRAWING. 2nd ed. Englewood Cliffs, New Jersey: Prentice-Hall, 1967.

Getzels, Jacob W. and Mihaly Csikszentmihalyi. CREATIVE
THINKING IN ART STUDENTS: AN EXPLORATORY STUDY.
Chicago: University of Chicago, 1964.

Groch, Judith. THE RIGHT TO CREATE. Boston: Little, Brown,
1970.

Hatcher, Evelyn P. "Navaho Art: a Methodological Study in
Visual Communication." Dissertation, University of Minnesota,
1967.

Havelka, Jaroslav. THE NATURE OF THE CREATIVE PROCESS
IN ART. A PSYCHOLOGICAL STUDY. The Hague: Martinus
Nijhoff, 1968. Review: BRITISH JOURNAL OF AESTHETICS
(Gordon Westland) pp. 89-90, January 9, 1969.

Kavolis, Vytautas. ARTISTIC EXPRESSION - A SOCIOLOGICAL
ANALYSIS. New York: Cornell University Press, 1968. Review:
BRITISH JOURNAL OF AESTHETICS (Michael Eastham) pp.
92-93, January 9, 1969.

Kepes, Gyorgy. LANGUAGE OF VISION. Chicago: Theobald, 1945.

Kepes, Gyorgy, ed. MAN MADE OBJECT. New York: G. Braziller,
1966.

Koestler, Arthur. THE ACT OF CREATION. London: Hutchitson,
1969. Review: REVIEW OF METAPHYSICS (Carl Ransdell
Hausman) pp. 88-112, September 20, 1966.

Lowenfeld, Viktor and W. Lambert Brittain. CREATIVE AND
MENTAL GROWTH. 5th ed. New York: MacMillan, 1970.

Lowenfeld, Viktor. THE NATURE OF CREATIVE ACTIVITY.
2nd ed. London: Routledge and Paul, 1952.

McKellar, Peter. IMAGINATION AND THINKING; A PSYCHOLOGI-
CAL ANALYSIS. New York: Basic Books, 1957.

Malraux, Andre. VOICES OF SILENCE. Garden City, New York: Doubleday, 1953.

Maritain, Jacques. CREATIVE INTUITION IN ART AND POETRY. New York: Meridian Books, 1955.

Merritt, Helen. GUIDING FREE EXPRESSION IN CHILDREN'S ART. New York: Holt, Rinehart and Winston, 1964.

Milner, Marion. ON NOT BEING ABLE TO PAINT. 2nd ed. New York: International Universities Press, 1957.

Nahm, Milton Charles. THE ARTIST AS CREATOR; AN ESSAY OF HUMAN FREEDOM. Baltimore: Johns Hopkins Press, 1956.

Osborn, Alexander Faickney. YOUR CREATIVE POWER: HOW TO USE IMAGINATION. New York: Scribner, 1948.

Pelles, Geraldine. ART, ARTISTS, AND SOCIETY: ORIGINS OF A MODERN DILEMMA. Englewood Cliffs, New Jersey: Prentice Hall, 1963.

Read, Herbert. ART AND SOCIETY. New York: Schocken Books, 1966.

Schaefer-Simmern, Henry. THE UNFOLDING OF ARTISTIC ACTIV-ITY, ITS BASIS, PROCESSES, AND IMPLICATIONS. Berkeley: University of California Press, 1961.

Sencourt, Robert. THE CONSECRATION OF GENIUS: AN ESSAY TO ELUCIDATE THE DISTINCTIVE SIGNIFICANCE AND QUAL-ITY OF CHRISTIAN ART BY ANALYSIS AND COMPARISON OF CERTAIN MASTERPIECES. London: Hollis and Carter, 1947.

Sorell, Walter. THE DUALITY OF VISION: GENIUS AND VERSATIL-ITY IN THE ARTS. Indianapolis: Bobbs-Merrill, 1970.

Stark, George King. AN ANALYSIS OF ARTIST-TEACHERS' STATEMENTS ON THEIR CREATIVITY. Ann Arbor, Michigan:

University Microfilms, 1961.

Sykes, Gerald. PERENNIAL AVANTGARDE. Englewood Cliffs, New Jersey: Prentice-Hall, 1971.

Tomas, Vincent, ed. CREATIVITY IN THE ARTS. Englewood Cliffs, New Jersey: Prentice-Hall, 1964.

Wilson, Frank Avray. ART AS UNDERSTANDING; A PAINTER'S ACCOUNT OF THE LAST REVOLUTION IN ART AND ITS BEARING ON HUMAN EXISTENCE AS A WHOLE. London: Routledge and K. Paul, 1963.

---. ART INTO LIFE: AN INTERPRETATION OF CONTEMPORARY TRENDS IN PAINTING. London: Centaur Press, 1958.

CREATIVITY IN EDUCATION

PERIODICALS

Anzalone, P. and D. Stahl. "Strategies For Creative Teaching." INSTRUCTOR 76:15-26, May, 1967.

Applegate, J. R. "Why Don't Pupils Talk in Class Discussions?" CLEARING HOUSE 44:78-81, October, 1969.

Armour, C. "Listen and Learn." TIMES EDUCATIONAL SUPPLEMENT 2817:1635, May 16, 1969.

Barbe, W. B. "Personalized Reading Program." EDUCATION 87: 33-36, September, 1966.

"Bates Creatives Help Kids With Writing Problem." ADVERTISING AGE 39:102, March 25, 1968.

"Block Island (a PACE project)." AMERICAN EDUCATION 2:9, November, 1966.

Boyle, R. P. "Functional Dilemmas In the Development of Learning" (bibliography). SOCIOLOGY OF EDUCATION 42:71-90, Winter, 1969.

Cobin, Martin T. "Criticism in Teaching: Oral Interpretation and Drama." WESTERN SPEECH JOURNAL 28:27-34, Winter, 1964.

Conway, J. A. "What Are We Rewarding?" (bibliography). PHI DELTA KAPPAN 51:87-89, October, 1969.

Cottle, T. J. "Bristol Township Schools: Strategy for Change."
SATURDAY REVIEW 52:70-71, September 20, 1969.

Covington, M. V. "Some Experimental Evidence on Teaching For
Creative Understanding." READING TEACHER 20:390-396,
February, 1967.

David, Brother Austin. "Teacher Education Through an Innovation of Modern Technology." NCEA BULLETIN 65:25-32,
May, 1969.

Edgar, T. "Invaluable By-product of Creativity." PHI DELTA
KAPPAN 46:273-276, February, 1965.

Edwards, M. O. "Fostering Creativity In a Liberal Arts College."
IMPROVING COLLEGE AND UNIVERSITY TEACHING 13:216-
219, Autumn, 1965.

Eiseman, R. "Creativity and Academic Major: Business Versus
English Majors" (bibliography). JOURNAL OF APPLIED
PSYCHOLOGY 53:392-395, October, 1969.

Eisner, E. W. "Think With Me About Creativity." INSTRUCTOR
72:3, September, 1962; p. 3, October, 1962; p. 3, November, 1962;
p. 3, December, 1962; p. 3, January, 1963; p. 5, February, 1963;
p. 5, March, 1963; p. 3, April, 1963; p. 3, May, 1963; p. 3, June,
1963.

Feldhasen, J. F. "Teaching Creative Thinking" (bibliography).
ELEMENTARY SCHOOL JOURNAL 70:48-53, October, 1969.

Fleck, H. "Creativity." PRACTICAL FORECAST FOR HOME
ECONOMICS 10:11, May, 1965.

Freedman, M. and others. "Utilizing Drug-experienced Youth In
Drug Education Programs, Silver Lake Regional High School,
Kingston, Mass." NATIONAL ASSOCIATION OF SECONDARY-
SCHOOL PRINCIPALS BULLETIN 53:45-51, September, 1969.

Education

Gallagher, J. J. "Meaningful Learning and Retention: Intrapersonal Cognitive Variables; Creativity." REVIEW OF EDUCATIONAL RESEARCH 34:503-505, December, 1964.

Garber, G. E. and S. L. French. "Closed Circuit Television Used To Train Teachers Of the Deaf." VOLTA REVIEW 71:362-366, September, 1969.

Gill, J. E. "ITV: Move Up or Move Out!" EDUCATIONAL SCREEN AND AUDIOVISUAL GUIDE 48:10-11, May, 1969.

Goldstein, I. "WSRS, a Radio-TV Station That Almost Is." GRADE TEACHER 87:124, October, 1969.

Goodman, P. and others. "Examination Of Some Measures of Creative Ability By the Multitrait Multimethod Matrix." JOURNAL OF APPLIED PSYCHOLOGY 53:240-243, June, 1969.

Goulet, R. R. "PACE & AV Communication." EDUCATIONAL SCREEN AND AUDIOVISUAL GUIDE 48:22-25, February, 1969; pp. 20-23, March, 1969.

Grey, A. "Creative Learning in Children's Playgrounds." CHILD-HOOD EDUCATION 45:491-499, May, 1969.

Grispino. "Crises Concerning Creativity." SCHOOL AND COMMUN-ITY 56:80-81, November, 1969.

Gross, L. S. "Utilizing ITV For Performance Classes (Junior colleges)." AUDIOVISUAL INSTRUCTION 14:54, November, 1969.

Harris, K. "Necessity For Nonconformity." MUSIC EDUCATORS JOURNAL 51:43-46, April, 1965.

Hearn, N. E. "Change For the Sake Of Change: Why Not? PACE: Projects To Advance Creativity in Education." NATIONAL ELEMENTARY PRINCIPAL 46:50-52, September, 1966.

The Communicative Arts

Hymes, J. L. "Fives: Creators and Innovators." GRADE TEACHER
80:15, January, 1963.

Jarzen, C. "Spark Within." OHIO SCHOOLS 43:14-16, December,
1965.

Johnson, D. W. and L. B. Johnson. "Intervention Within Uncry-
stallized Groups." EDUCATIONAL LEADERSHIP 27:39-41,
October, 1969.

Kase, J. B. "Theatre Resources For Youth In New Hampshire:
PACE Project." EDUCATIONAL THEATRE JOURNAL 21:205-
213, May, 1969.

Katz, S. F. "Turning the Kids On With Media." AUDIOVISUAL
INSTRUCTION 14:48-51, October, 1969.

Keller, F. A. "Upstart Arts." SCHOOL ARTS 59:9-14, June, 1960.

Kingsley, W. "Controversial Compton Concept Shapes CTA
Position On Television." CALIFORNIA TEACHERS ASSOCIA-
TION JOURNAL 57:10, January, 1961.

Lewis, C. "Conference Group Leader; a Model?" JOURNAL OF
TEACHER EDUCATION 20:61-65, Spring, 1969.

Lewis, G. M. "Releasing Creativity" (bibliography). CHILDHOOD
EDUCATION 41:295-300, February, 1965.

Litsey, D. M. "Small-group Training and The English Classroom." ENGLISH JOURNAL 58:920-927, September, 1969.

McCavitt, W. "Educational Radio--Star On the Rise." PENNSYL-
VANIA SCHOOL JOURNAL p. 115, April, 1967.

Macchiarola, F. J. and J. T. Skerrett, Jr. "Creative Dialogue In
the Classroom: the Technology Of Teaching." CATHOLIC
EDUCATIONAL REVIEW 66:376-390, September, 1968.

34

Education

McClerren, B. F. "Creative Teaching." SPEECH TEACHER 15: 212-216, September, 1966.

McCreary, E. "Schools For Fearlessness and Freedom." PHI DELTA KAPPAN 46:257-267, February, 1965.

MacLeod, J. "Sensitivity Training, What's That? Is It For a Local Church?" INTERNATIONAL JOURNAL OF RELIGIOUS EDUCATION 43:8-9, December, 1966.

McMahan, M. "Mini Courses; a Method For Teacher Education." AUDIOVISUAL INSTRUCTION 14:66, June, 1969.

Monts, E. A. and B. H. Peterson. "Graduate Teaching By Telephone and Radio." JOURNAL OF HOME ECONOMICS 61:443-447, June, 1969.

Myers, B. J. "We Produce a Radio Unit." SCHOOL ACTIVITIES 32:67-68, November, 1969.

Nelson, L. "Developing the Creative Process and Product" (bibliography). NATIONAL ELEMENTARY PRINCIPAL 44:35-39, May, 1965.

Norris, R. C. "Texas Educational Microwave Project." SCHOOL LIFE 45:11-13, January, 1963.

Norwood, F. W. "Telecommunications, the Total Medium." EDUCATIONAL SCREEN AND AUDIOVISUAL GUIDE 48:14-15, May, 1969.

Otte, R. W. "Creativity In Teaching." CHILDHOOD EDUCATION 43:40-43, September, 1966.

Oyer, H. J. "Teaching Lipreading By Television" (bibliography). VOLTA REVIEW 63:131-132, 141, March, 1961.

"PACE Provides For Imaginative Solutions." MINNESOTA JOURNAL OF EDUCATION 47:32, February, 1967.

Peterson, P. G. "Creativity vs. the Profit Motive." AUDIO-
VISUAL INSTRUCTION 10:386-387, September, 1964.

Rawley, P. "Serious U. S. TV Fights For Life." NEW STATESMAN
77:500-501, April 11, 1969.

Ray, H. W. "Freeing Pupils From the Sit-Look-Listen Syndrome."
NEA JOURNAL 56:8-10, April, 1967.

Rigby, W. H. and R. H. Fricker. "Boob Tube Goes To High
School." INDUSTRIAL ARTS AND VOCATIONAL EDUCATION
58:34-35, June, 1969.

Scholl, S. "Cultivation Of Creativity." PEABODY JOURNAL OF
EDUCATION 44:282-285, March, 1967.

Seaberg, S. "You Have Nothing To Lose But Your Phobias!"
JOURNAL OF SECONDARY EDUCATION 42:147-150, April,
1967.

Seitz, J. E. "Creative Problem Solving." SCHOOL SHOP 26:66-69,
March, 1967.

"Sensitivity Training: Can It Work For the Schools?" NATIONS
SCHOOLS 83:83-87, March, 1969.

Shores, Louis. "The Junior College Impact On Academic
Librarianship. (The innovative college I have in mind...The
community college has dared to break with some sacred tra-
ditions of higher education...p. 215)." COLLEGE AND RE-
SEARCH LIBRARIES 30:214-221, May, 1969.

Taylor, C. W. "Instructional Media and Creativity." AUDIO-
VISUAL INSTRUCTION 7:376-377, June, 1963.

Thoresen, C. E. "Video In the College Classroom: an Exploratory
Study" (bibliography). PERSONNEL AND GUIDANCE JOURNAL
45:144-149, October, 1966.

Torrance, E .P. "Uniqueness and Creativeness: the School's Role." EDUCATIONAL LEADERSHIP 24:493-496, March, 1967.

Veatch, J. and G. Hayes. "Individualizing Instruction; Some Classroom-tested Ideas." NEA JOURNAL 55:38, November, 1966.

Wagner, G. "What Schools Are Doing; Fostering Creativity " (bibliography). EDUCATION 86:440-443, March, 1966.

Williams, M. G. "Teaching With TV: One Of History's Marvels." IMPROVING COLLEGE AND UNIVERSITY TEACHING 17:118-119, Spring, 1969.

Wilson, L. S. "Inservice Training; Lifeline For Integration." NATIONS SCHOOLS 84:70-71, October, 1969.

Witty, P. A. "Recent Publications Concerning the Gifted and Creative Student" (bibliography). PHI DELTA KAPPAN 46:221-224, January, 1965.

Wolfson, B. J. "Creativity In the Classroom" (bibliography). ELEMENTARY ENGLISH 38:523-524, November, 1961.

"Workshop: How To Use Television More Effectively, Williamsville and Buffalo, N.Y." SCHOOL MANAGEMENT 13:21, October, 1969.

Yamamoto, K. "Mental Health, Creative Thinking and Values" (bibliography). ELEMENTARY SCHOOL JOURNAL 66:361-367, April, 1966.

Ziller, R. C. "Group Creativity Under Conditions of Success or Failure and Variations in Group Stability" (bibliography). JOURNAL OF APPLIED PSYCHOLOGY 46:43-49, February, 1962.

BOOKS

ALERT, A SOURCEBOOK OF ELEMENTARY CURRICULA PRO-
GRAMS AND PROJECTS. Washington, D.C.: Government Printing
Office, 1972.

Freeman, James and others. CREATIVITY: A SELECTIVE REVIEW
OF RESEARCH. London: Society for Research into Higher Education, Limited, 1971.

Wertheimer, Max. PRODUCTIVE THINKING. New York: Harper,
1959.

CREATIVITY IN FICTION

PERIODICALS

Adams, J. Donald. "Does Anyone Know What Creative Writing Is?" SATURDAY REVIEW 48:23-25, September 18, 1965.

Asimov, Issac. "SF: Clue to Creativity." LIBRARY JOURNAL 89:914-917, February 15, 1964.

Balakian, Nona. "The Prophetic Vogue of the Anti-Heroine." SOUTHWEST REVIEW 47:134-141, Spring, 1962.

Beja, Morris. "It Must Be Important: Negroes in Contemporary American Fiction." ANTIOCH REVIEW 24:323-336, Fall, 1964.

Bezanker, Abraham. "Odyssey of Saul Bellow." YALE REVIEW 58:359-371, Spring, 1969.

"Black Humorists." TIME 85:94-96, February 12, 1965.

Boyers, Robert. "Attitudes Toward Sex in American 'High Culture'." ANNALS OF THE AMERICAN ACADEMY OF POLITICAL AND SOCIAL SCIENCE 376:36-52, March, 1968.

Brossard, Chandler. "Ritual of Originality." NATION 206:575-576, April 29, 1968.

Burgess, Anthony. "Language, Myth and Mr. Updike." COMMONWEAL 83:557-559, February 11, 1966.

Capon, Robert T. "Herzog and the Passion." AMERICA

112:425-427, March 27, 1965.

Capouya, Emile. "Crisis in Creativity." SATURDAY REVIEW 48:32-34, August 31, 1965.

Case, L. L. "Yet Another Interview with B. Bonnet: Fiction as Nonfiction." NATION 202:193-194, February 14, 1966.

Conquest, Robert. "Science Fiction and Literature." CRITICAL QUARTERLY 5:355-367, Winter, 1963.

Cowley, Malcolm. "Personalism: A New School of Fiction." NEW REPUBLIC 131:16-18, October 18, 1954.

---. "Tidy Room in Bedlam; Notes on the New Fiction." HARPER'S MAGAZINE 206:27-33, April, 1953.

Craig, Eugene A. "Psychology of Creative Writing." WRITER 76: 15-17, August, 1963.

Crichton, J. Michael. "Sci-Fi and Vonnegut." NEW REPUBLIC 160:33-35, April 26, 1969.

Curley, Thomas F. "Catholic Novels and American Culture." COMMENTARY 36:34-42, July, 1963.

deLissovoy, Peter. "Visible Ellison." NATION 199:334-336, November 9, 1964.

Elliott, George P. "Exploring the Province of the Short Story." HARPER'S MAGAZINE 230:111-116, April, 1965.

---. "Hurtsog, Hairtsog, Heart's Hog?" NATION 199:252-254, October 19, 1964.

Ely, Sister M. Amanda. "The Adult Image in Three Novels of Adolescent Life." ENGLISH JOURNAL 56:1127-1131, November, 1967.

Fiction

Enright, D. J. "Updike's Ups and Downs." HOLIDAY 38:162, 164-166, November, 1965.

Featherstone, Joseph. "Katherine Anne Porter's Harvest." NEW REPUBLIC 153:23-26, September 4, 1965.

Fleming, Thomas J. "Novel of the Future." AMERICA 114:654-655, 658, May 7, 1966.

"Future of Fiction." PUBLISHER'S WEEKLY 195:32, March 24, 1969.

Galloway, David D. "Clown and Saint: The Hero in Current American Fiction." CRITIQUE 7:46-65, Spring-Summer, 1965.

Garis, Robert. "What Happened to John Barth?" COMMENTARY 42:89-90, 92, 94-95, October, 1966.

Geismar, Maxwell. "The American Short Story Today." STUDIES ON THE LEFT 4:21-27, Spring, 1964.

Gerhardt, Mia I. "Homocide West: Some Observations on the Nero Wolfe Stories of Rex Stout." ENGLISH STUDIES 49:107-127, April, 1968.

Gold, Herbert. "Fiction of the Sixties." ATLANTIC MONTHLY 206:53-57, September, 1960.

---. "United States." KENYON REVIEW 30,4:450-453, 1968.

Greenberg, Alvin. "The Novel of Disintegration: Paradoxical Impossibility in Contemporary Fiction." WISCONSIN STUDIES IN CONTEMPORARY LITERATURE 7:103-124, Winter-Spring, 1966.

Gross, Robert A. "The Black Novelists: 'Our Turn'." NEWSWEEK 73:94, 96B, 98, 100, June 16, 1969.

Grumbach, Doris. "On Women Novelists." COMMONWEAL 80:198-200, May 8, 1964.

Hale, Nancy. "Magic of Creativity." SATURDAY EVENING POST 234:24-25, 69-71, April 29, 1961.

Hartman, Geoffrey H. "Heroics of Realism." YALE REVIEW 53: 26-35, Autumn, 1963.

Hassan, Ihab. "Avant-garde: Which Way Is Forward?" NATION 193:396-399, November 18, 1961.

---. "The Character of Post-War Fiction in America." ENGLISH JOURNAL 51:1-8, January, 1962.

---. "Laughter in the Dark: The New Voice in American Fiction." AMERICAN SCHOLAR 33:636-638, 640, Autumn, 1964.

Hicks, Granville. "The Novel: Tradition vs. Experiment." SATURDAY REVIEW 51:27-28, February 10, 1968.

---. "Signatures to the Significance of the Self." SATURDAY RE- VIEW 47:67-70, 72, August 29, 1964.

---. "They Also Serve Who Write Well." SATURDAY REVIEW 48:25-26, May 15, 1965.

Hoffman, Michael J. "From Cohn to Herzog." YALE REVIEW 58:342-358, Spring, 1969.

Hoffman, Stanton. "The Cities of Night: John Rechy's CITY OF NIGHT and the American Literature of Homosex- uality." CHICAGO REVIEW 17,2-3:195-206, 1964.

Hofstadter, Beatrice K. "Popular Culture and the Romantic Heroine." AMERICAN SCHOLAR 30:98-116, Winter, 1960-1961.

Howe, Irving. "Fiction of Anti-Utopia." NEW REPUBLIC 146:13-16, April 23, 1962.

---. "Novels of the Post-War World." NEW REPUBLIC 139:16-18, November 10, 1958.

Fiction

"The Inspirational Value of Science Fiction." SCIENCE DIGEST
53:34, March, 1963.

Jones, Archie H. "Cops, Robbers, Heroes and Anti-Heroines: The
American Need to Create." JOURNAL OF POPULAR CULTURE
1:114-125, Fall, 1967.

Kauffman, Stanley. "Greatness as a Literary Standard." HARPER'S
MAGAZINE 231:151-156, November, 1965.

Kenkel, William F. "Marriage and the Family in Modern Science
Fiction." JOURNAL OF MARRIAGE AND THE FAMILY 31:6-14,
February, 1969.

Kersnowski, Frank L. "Exit the Anti-Hero." CRITIQUE 10,3:
60-71, 1968.

Levine, Paul. "The Intemperate Zone: The Climate of Contemporary
American Fiction." MASSACHUSETTS REVIEW 8:505-523,
Summer, 1967.

McIntyre, John P. "The Modes of Disillusionment: Irony in Modern
Fiction." RENASCENCE 17:70-76, 96, Winter, 1964.

Mailer, Norman. "Modes and Mutations: Quick Comments on the
Modern American Novel." COMMENTARY 41:37-40, March, 1966.

Marshall, Lenore. "What's Missing in the Novel." SATURDAY
REVIEW 46:15-16, February 9, 1963.

Michelson, Peter. "Pop Goes America; Absurdity in Literature."
NEW REPUBLIC 157:23-26, 28, September 9, 1967.

Morris, Robert K. "James Purdy and the Works." NATION 205:
342-344, October 9, 1967.

Morris, Wright. "Death of the Reader." NATION 198:53-54,
January 13, 1964.

43

"Obsessed with the Small." CHRISTIAN CENTURY 78:227-228, February 22, 1961.

Osterweis, Rollyn. "Pictures as Inspiration for Creativity." ENGLISH JOURNAL 57:93-95, January, 1968.

Patterson, Elizabeth Gregg. "If It's Shocking, Will It Sell?" WRITER 76:17-19, July, 1963.

Phillips, John. "Styron Unlocked." VOGUE 150:216-217, 267-271, 278, December, 1967.

Phillips, William. "Notes on the New Style." NATION 201:232-236, September 20, 1965.

"Predicts Puritan Revolution." CHRISTIAN CENTURY 81:1076-1077, September 2, 1964.

Raines, Charles. "Writer and the Common World." LIBRARY JOURNAL 90:1622, April 1, 1965.

Roth, Philip. "Writing American Fiction." COMMENTARY 31:223-233, March, 1961.

Rovit, Earl H. "The Ambiguous Modern Novel." YALE REVIEW 49:413-424, Spring, 1960.

---. "Fathers and Sons in American Fiction." YALE REVIEW 53:248-257, Winter, 1963.

Schickel, Richard. "Black Comedy with Purifying Laughter." HARPER'S MAGAZINE 232:103-104, 106, May, 1966.

Sheed, Wilfrid. "Jones Boy Forever." ATLANTIC MONTHLY 219:68-72, June, 1967.

Sisk, John P. "Confessional Hero." COMMONWEAL 72:167-170, May 13, 1960.

Fiction

Sklar, Robert. "The New Novel, USA: Thomas Pynchon." NATION 205:277-280, September, 1967.

Slaughter, Frank G. "Confessions of a Storyteller." ALA BULLE-TIN 59:1003-1005, December, 1965.

Smith, William James. "Pop Art and the Short Story." COMMON-WEAL 80:508-510, July 24, 1964.

Stafford, Jean. "Truth in Fiction." LIBRARY JOURNAL 91:4557-4565, October 1, 1966.

Stone, Emily Whitehurst. "How a Writer Finds His Material." HARPER'S MAGAZINE 231:157-161, November, 1965.

Sutton, Henry. "Notes Toward the Destruction of Culture." KENYON REVIEW 30:108-115, June 1, 1968.

Thody, Philip. "Sociology of Literary Creativity; a Literary Critic's View." INTERNATIONAL SOCIAL SCIENCE JOURNAL 20,3:487-498, 1968.

Updike, John. "Books; More Love in the Western World." NEW YORKER 39:90-94, 97-104, August 24, 1963.

Warren, Robert Penn. "Uncorrupted Consciousness: The Stories of Katherine Anne Porter." YALE REVIEW 55:280-290, Winter, 1966.

Welty, Eudora. "The Eye of the Story." YALE REVIEW 55: 265-274, Winter, 1966.

---. "Must the Novelist Crusade?" ATLANTIC MONTHLY 216:104-108, October, 1965.

West, Rebecca. "A Grave and Reverend Book." HARPER'S MAGAZINE 232:108, 110, 112-114, February, 1966.

Wiegand, William. "The 'Non-Fiction' Novel." NEW MEXICO

The Communicative Arts

QUARTERLY 37:243-257, Autumn, 1967.

Wolfe, Tom. "Pause, Now, and Consider Some Tentative Conclusions about Porno-Violence." ESQUIRE 68:59, 110, 112, July, 1967.

Yaffe, James. "The Modern Trend Toward Meaningful Martians." SATURDAY REVIEW 43:22-23, April 23, 1960.

THE WRITER. 1887-   . (A monthly periodical devoted to communication in literary writing)

Yglesias, Jose. "Coupling Uncoupling." NATION 206:637-638, May 13, 1968.

---. "Marx as Muse." NATION 200:368-370, April 5, 1965.

BOOKS

Aldridge, John W. TIME TO MURDER AND CREATE. New York: McKay, 1966.

Alvarez, Alfred. UNDER PRESSURE; THE WRITER IN SOCIETY: EASTERN EUROPE AND THE U.S.A. Baltimore: Penguin Books, 1965.

Birney, Earle. THE CREATIVE WRITER. Toronto: Canadian Broadcasting Corporation, 1966.

Bone, Robert A. THE NEGRO NOVEL IN AMERICA. Rev. ed. New Haven: Yale University Press, 1965.

Booth, Wayne. THE RHETORIC OF FICTION. Chicago: University of Chicago Press, 1961.

Fiction

Brace, Gerald Warner. THE STUFF OF FICTION. New York: Norton, 1969.

Brashers, Howard Charles. CREATIVE WRITING; FICTION, DRAMA, POETRY AND THE ESSAY. New York: American Book Company, 1968.

Cary, Joyce. ART AND REALITY: WAYS OF THE CREATIVE PROCESS. New York: Harper, 1958.

Cook, Albert Spaulding. THE MEANING OF FICTION. Detroit: Wayne State University Press, 1960.

Davis, Robert Murray. THE NOVEL: MODERN ESSAYS IN CRITI-CISM. Englewood Cliffs, New Jersey: Prentice-Hall, 1969.

Duff, William. AN ESSAY ON ORIGINAL GENIUS. New York: Garland Publishing Company, 1970.

Egri, Lajos. THE ART OF CREATIVE WRITING. New York: Citadel Press, 1965.

Ellmann, Mary. THINKING ABOUT WOMEN. New York: Harcourt, Brace and World, 1968.

Fiedler, Leslie A. LOVE AND DEATH IN THE AMERICAN NOVEL. 2nd ed. New York: Stein and Day, 1966.

Halprin, Lawrence. THE RSVP CYCLES; CREATIVE PROCESSES IN THE HUMAN ENVIRONMENT. New York: G. Braziller, 1970.

Harding, Denys Clement Wyatt. EXPERIENCE INTO WORDS. New York: Horizon Press, 1964.

Harper, Howard M. DESPARATE FAITH: A STUDY OF BELLOW, SALINGER, MAILER, BALDWIN, AND UPDIKE. Chapel Hill: University of North Carolina Press, 1967.

Harper, Ralph. THE WORLD OF THE THRILLER. Cleveland:

Press of Case Western Reserve University, 1969.

Hassan, Ihab. RADICAL INNOCENCE: STUDIES IN THE CONTEM-
PORARY AMERICAN NOVEL. Princeton, New Jersey: Princeton
University Press, 1961.

Hill, Herbert, ed. ANGER, AND BEYOND: THE NEGRO WRITER IN
THE UNITED STATES. New York: Harper and Row, 1966.

Hillegas, Mark Robert, ed. SHADOWS OF IMAGINATION; THE
FANTASIES OF C. S. LEWIS, J. R. R. TOLKIEN, AND CHARLES
WILLIAMS. Carbondale: Southern Illinois University Press, 1969.

Hoffman, Frederick John. THE IMAGINATION'S NEW BEGINNING:
THEOLOGY AND MODERN LITERATURE. Notre Dame,
Indiana: University of Notre Dame Press, 1967.

Jellema, Roderick, ed. CONTEMPORARY WRITERS IN CHRISTIAN
PERSPECTIVE. Grand Rapids, Michigan: William B. Eerdmans
Publishing Company, 1966-   . (A continuing series of mono-
graphs on modern and contemporary writers)

Jones, Howard Mumford. BELIEF AND DISBELIEF IN AMERICAN
LITERATURE. Chicago: University of Chicago Press, 1967.

Kaplan, Harold J. THE PASSIVE VOICE; AN APPROACH TO
MODERN FICTION. Athens: Ohio University Press, 1966.

Klein, Marcus. AFTER ALIENATION: AMERICAN NOVELS IN MID-
CENTURY. Cleveland: World, 1965.

---. THE AMERICAN NOVEL SINCE WORLD WAR II. Greenwich,
Connecticut: Fawcett Publications, Incorporated, 1969.

Koestler, Arthur. ACT OF CREATION. London: Hutchinson, 1964.

Kosinski, Leonard V., ed. READINGS ON CREATIVITY AND
IMAGINATION IN LITERATURE AND LANGUAGE. Champaign,
Illinois: National Council of Teachers of English, 1968.

Fiction

Krieger, Murray. THE TRAGIC VISION: VARIATIONS ON A THEME
IN LITERARY INTERPRETATION. New York: Holt, Rinehart and
Winston, 1960.

Kiehl, John Richard. CREATIVE WRITING AND REWRITING;
CONTEMPORARY AMERICAN NOVELISTS AT WORK. New
York: Appleton-Century-Crofts, 1967.

---. WRITE AND REWRITE: A STUDY OF THE CREATIVE PRO-
CESS. New York: Meredith Press, 1967.

Leavitt, Hart Day. THE WRITER'S EYE. New York: Bantam
Books, 1968.

Lyons, John O. THE COLLEGE NOVEL IN AMERICA. Carbondale:
Southern Illinois University Press, 1962.

Malin, Irving. NEW AMERICAN GOTHIC. Carbondale: Southern
Illinois University Press, 1962.

Mathieu, Aron M., ed. THE CREATIVE WRITER. Rev. ed.
Cincinnati: Writer's Digest, 1968.

Meredith, Robert C. THE PROFESSIONAL STORY WRITER AND
HIS ART. New York: Crowell, 1963.

Moore, Harry T., ed. CONTEMPORARY AMERICAN NOVELISTS.
Carbondale: Southern Illinois University Press, 1964.

Peden, William. THE AMERICAN SHORT STORY: FRONT LINE
IN THE NATIONAL DEFENSE OF LITERATURE. Boston:
Houghton, Mifflin, 1964.

Podhoretz, Norman. DOINGS AND UNDOINGS: THE FIFTIES AND
AFTER IN AMERICAN WRITING. New York: Farrar, Straus, 1964.

Ruitenbeek, Hendrik Marinus, ed. THE LITERARY IMAGINATION:
PSYCHO-ANALYSIS AND THE GENIUS OF THE WRITER.
Chicago: Quadrangle Books, 1965.

Rupp, Richard H. CELEBRATION IN POSTWAR AMERICAN
FICTION. Coral Gables, Florida: University of Miami Press,
1970.

Scholes, Robert. THE FABULATORS. New York: Oxford University Press, 1967.

--- and Robert Kellogg. THE NATURE OF NARRATIVE. New
York: Oxford University Press, 1966.

Schulz, Max F. RADICAL SOPHISTICATION: STUDIES IN CONTEM-
PORARY JEWISH-AMERICAN NOVELISTS. Athens: Ohio University Press, 1969.

Sen Gupta, Subodh Chandra. TOWARDS A THEORY OF THE
IMAGINATION. Bombay: Indian Branch, Oxford University
Press, 1959.

Spearman, Diana. THE NOVEL AND SOCIETY. New York: Barnes
and Noble, 1966.

Stevick, Philip. THE THEORY OF THE NOVEL. New York: The
Free Press, 1967.

Van Nostrand, Albert. THE DENATURED NOVEL. Indianapolis:
Bobbs-Merrill, 1960.

Weinberg, Helen. THE NEW NOVEL: THE KAFKAN MODE IN
CONTEMPORARY FICTION. Ithaca: Cornell University Press,
1970.

CREATIVITY IN FILMS

PERIODICALS

Alpert, H. "Film of Social Reality." SATURDAY REVIEW OF LITERATURE 52:43-44, September 6, 1969.

"Art of Light and Lunace: The New Underground Films." TIME 89:94-99, February 17, 1967.

"Art that matters: A Look at Today's Film Scene by the Under-thirties; Symposium." SATURDAY REVIEW OF LITERATURE 52:7-11, 36, December 27, 1969.

Banner, W. P. "Fps Creativity." U. S. CAMERA 28:72-73, 87, July, 1965.

Barrios, G. "Naming names: the Films of Carl Linder." FILM QUARTERLY 22:41-46, Fall, 1968.

Bunzel, P. "Outbreak of New Films For Adults Only." LIFE 52: 88-96, February 23, 1962.

Colimore, B. "Trying to Breathe Underground." CATHOLIC WORLD 207:119-123, June, 1968.

"Electronovision; John Gielgud's production of HAMLET on Film." AMERICA 111:28, July 11, 1964.

Farber, P. "Wein Sound Trigger." TRAVEL AND CAMERA 32: 47-48, February, 1969.

"Festival I; Experiments Of Film-makers' Cinematheque." NEW YORKER 41:52-54, December 4, 1965.

Ford, B. "Underground-movie Thing." SCIENCE DIGEST 65:52-54, June, 1969.

Garis, R. "Art-movie Style." COMMENTARY 44:77-79, August, 1967.

Gill, B. "Current Cinema: Underground Movies." NEW YORKER 42:130-132, April 23, 1966.

Gordon, M. W. "What Film Making Is All About." AMERICA 121: 555-557, December 6, 1969.

Kael, P. "So Off-beat We Lose the Beat." NEW REPUBLIC 155:42-45, November 5, 1966.

---. "Trash, Art, and the Movies." HARPER'S MAGAZINE 238:65-68, February, 1969.

Knight, A. "G as in Good Entertainment." SATURDAY REVIEW OF LITERATURE 52:40, March 1, 1969.

---. "Marshaling McLuhanism; Exhibits at Expo 67." SATURDAY REVIEW OF LITERATURE 50:41-42, 46, August 12, 1967.

Kroll, J. "Up from Underground." NEWSWEEK 69:117-119, February 13, 1967.

Lapham, L. H. "Freely Is Here: Sensorama Simulator." SATURDAY EVENING POST 237:28-29, April 18, 1964.

Lynch, W. F. "Counter Revolution In the Movies." COMMONWEAL 87:77-79, October 20, 1967.

MacDonald, D. "Films: Bad Good Movies." ESQUIRE 65:44, June, 1966.

Films

Mann, M. "Foothill Film Festival; Running People, Symbolic Seagulls." POPULAR PHOTOGRAPHY 65:26, October, 1969.

Mapes, Glynn. "Middlebrows Wanted: Educational TV offers More Programs With Broader Appeal; Stations Air Sports, Movies, Popular Drama To Build Up Audiences, Cash Donation." WALL STREET JOURNAL 167:1, January 4, 1966.

Matzkin, M. A. "Matzkin on Movies; Forget the Conventions." MODERN PHOTOGRAPHY 31:30, January, 1967.

"Movie You Feel and Smell As Well As See." POPULAR SCIENCE 187:44-45, July, 1965.

Nathan, P. "Rights and Permissions; Predictions In 1924 by D. W. Griffith." PUBLISHERS' WEEKLY 192:71, November 13, 1967.

Penn, Stanley. "The Golden Screen: United Artists Corporation Takes Lead in Movie Industry Backing Independents." WALL STREET JOURNAL 167:1, May 9, 1966.

"Saying It On Film: Teen Movie-making." SEVENTEEN 23:162-163, April, 1964.

Skow, J. "Small War In Westport; Amateur Moviemakers Are Waging World War I." SATURDAY EVENING POST 237:18-19, November 28, 1964.

"Spoofing the Spooks." NEWSWEEK 53:98, April 6, 1959.

Trevelyan, C. F. "Slapstick To Satire." U. S. CAMERA 29:70-73, September, 1966.

"Up From the Underground." NEWSWEEK 67:90, April 25, 1966.

Wagner, G. "Movies: Avant-garde Films." NATIONAL REVIEW 16:502-503, June 16, 1964.

Wildi, E. "Consider the Audience." U. S. CAMERA 29:68-69, 74,

The Communicative Arts

July, 1966.

BOOKS

Renan, Sheldon. AN INTRODUCTION TO THE AMERICAN UNDER-GROUND FILM. New York: Dutton, 1967.

CREATIVITY IN GROUP COMMUNICATION

PERIODICALS

Alker, H. A. and N. Kogan. "Effects of Norm-oriented Group Discussion on Individual Verbal Risk Taking and Conservatism." HUMAN RELATIONS 21:393-405, November, 1968.

Banta, T. W. and J. E. McCormick. "Using the Leaderless Group Discussion Technique for Selection of Residence Hall Counselors." NATIONAL ASSOCIATION WOMEN DEANS AND COUNSELORS JOURNAL 33:30-33, Fall, 1969.

Birnbaum, M. "Sense about Sensitivity Training." SATURDAY REVIEW 52:82-83, 96-98, November 15, 1969.

Blank, L. and others. "Intense Encounters in Human Relations Training." PERSONNEL AND GUIDANCE JOURNAL 48:56-57, September, 1969.

Brown, R. L. "Creative Process in the Popular Arts." INTERNATIONAL SOCIAL SCIENCE JOURNAL 20,4:613-624, 1968.

Buchman, S. J. "Creativity and Coordination." PULP AND PAPER 41:40-43, May 1, 1967.

Cain, M. E. "Some Suggested Developments For Role and Reference Group Analysis" (bibliography). BRITISH JOURNAL OF SOCIOLOGY 19:191-205, June, 1968.

Calsbeek, F. "Brainstorming Health Problems; a Creative Approach." JOURNAL OF SCHOOL HEALTH 38:530-532, October,

1968.

Cartwright, D. "Risk Taking By Individuals and Groups: An Assessment of Research Employing Choice Dilemmas." JOURNAL OF PERSONALITY AND SOCIAL PHYCHOLOGY 20:361-378, 1971.

Cassels, L. "Eight Keys to Creativity; How to Identify Imaginative Workers " (Penn State Research). NATIONS BUSINESS 47:58-59, February, 1959.

Collaros, P. A. and L. R. Anderson. "Effect of Perceived Expertness Upon Creativity of Members of Brainstorming Groups" (bibliography). JOURNAL OF APPLIED PSYCHOLOGY 53:159-163, April, 1969.

Coopersmith, Stanley. "Studies in Self-Esteem." SCIENTIFIC AMERICAN 219:96-106, February, 1968.

"Creativity, Communication and the Lack of Both." SALES MANAGEMENT 102:86, April 15, 1969.

Dauw, D. C. "Creativity and Vocational Needs of Clerical Personnel." PERSONNEL JOURNAL 47:870-876, December, 1968.

Deep, S. D. and others. "Some Effects on Business Gaming of Previous Quasi-T Group Affiliations." JOURNAL OF APPLIED PSYCHOLOGY 51:426-431, October, 1967.

Elenko, W. "Business Administration Think-in and Speak Out." JOURNAL OF BUSINESS EDUCATION 44:245-246, March, 1969.

Feinberg, M. R. "Fourteen Suggestions for Managing Scientific Creativity" (bibliography). RESEARCH MANAGEMENT 11:83-92, March, 1968.

Fitch, James M. "The Control of the Luminous Environment (Architecture)." SCIENTIFIC AMERICAN 219:191, September, 1968.

Fleck, H. "T-Group." FORECAST FOR HOME ECONOMICS 12: 15, January, 1967.

Fourastie, J. "America's Amazing Power to Create." ATLAS 15:15, January, 1967.

Friedlander, F. "Performance and Interactional Dimensions of Organizational Work Groups" (bibliography). JOURNAL OF APPLIED PSYCHOLOGY 50:257-265, June, 1966.

Friedman, J. J. "Are you Creative?" DUNS REVIEW AND MODERN INDUSTRY 79:63-64, May, 1962.

Geier, J. G. "Trait Approach to the Study of Leadership in Small Groups." JOURNAL OF COMMUNICATION 17:316-323, December, 1967.

Gray, C. E. "Measurement of Creativity in Western Civilization" (bibliography). AMERICAN ANTHROPOLOGIST 68:1384-1417, December, 1968.

Hartley, J. and N. Beasley. "Contrary Imaginations at Keele" (bibliography). UNIVERSITIES QUARTERLY 23:467-471, Autumn, 1969.

"How to Mass Produce Creativity." MANAGEMENT METHODS 19:52-54, February, 1961.

"Identify Your Creative People." NATIONS BUSINESS 46:48, September, 1958.

Jackson, E. W. "Hunting Yardsticks for Creativity." MANAGEMENT REVIEW 54:38-41, March, 1965.

Joyce, B. and others. "Sensitivity Training for Teachers: An Experiment" (bibliography). JOURNAL OF TEACHER EDUCATION 20:75-83, Spring, 1969.

Kemper, T. P. "Reference Groups, Socialization and Achievement."

AMERICAN SOCIOLOGICAL REVIEW 33:31-45, February, 1968.

Klingsick, J. "Ideas in Motion Youth Theater: A Growing Expression of Creativity." YOUNG CHILDREN 23:324-328, September, 1968.

Lahti, A. K. "Are We Really Ready for Creativity?" PERSONNEL ADMINISTRATION 27:20-23, March, 1964.

Mial, D. J. and S. Jacobson. "Brainstorming." TODAYS EDUCATION 57:68, 80, November, 1968.

---. "Fishbowl; Design for Discussion." TODAYS EDUCATION 57:28-29, September, 1968.

Moe, E. "Towns Group: The Media to Promote Pupil Creativity." AUDIOVISUAL INSTRUCTION 9:434-435, September, 1964.

Monaghan, R. R. "A Systematic Way of Being Creative." JOURNAL OF COMMUNICATION 18:47-56, March, 1968.

Moore, E. O. "Where Do New Ideas Come From?" INTERNATIONAL JOURNAL OF RELIGIOUS EDUCATION 44:10-11, September, 1968.

Mueller, L. "Concrete Poetry: Creative Writing for All Students" (bibliography). ENGLISH JOURNAL 58:1053-1056, October, 1969.

Nicholson, P. J. "Step Up Your Flow Of Ideas. Creativity Extends Well Beyond Domain of Intelligence ." PUBLIC RELATIONS JOURNAL 16:12-14, August, 1960.

Otto, H. A. "Depth Unfoldment Experience; A Method for Creating Interpersonal Closeness." ADULT EDUCATION 17:78-84, Winter, 1967.

Prickett, E. "These Kids Tell Whoppers and Learn." GRADE TEACHER 87:130-134, September, 1969.

Pruitt, D. G. "Choice Shifts in Group Discussion: An Introductory Review." JOURNAL OF PERSONALITY AND SOCIAL PSYCHOLOGY 20:339-360, 1971.

---. "Conclusions: Toward an Understanding of Choice Shifts in Group Discussion." JOURNAL OF PERSONALITY AND SOCIAL PSYCHOLOGY 20:495-510, 1971.

Richstone, M. "Six Weeks' Brainstorming for Creativity." INSTRUCTOR 78:64, August, 1968.

Rinn, J. L. "Dimensions of Group Interaction: The Cooperative Analysis of Idosyncratic Descriptions of Training Groups" (bibliography). EDUCATIONAL AND PSYCHOLOGICAL MEASUREMENT 26:343-362, Summer, 1966.

Shaimin, D. "Problem Solving Goes Creative." ADMINISTRATIVE MANAGEMENT 30:30-31, August, 1969.

Sigut, W. and R. Lohr. "Teacher Sensitivity Groups." PENNSYLVANIA SCHOOL JOURNAL 118:30, September, 1969.

Silverstein, L. "Word Game." PHI DELTA KAPPAN 50:466-467, April, 1969.

Skipper, C. E. and J. A. DeVelbiss. "Developing Creative Abilities in Adolescence; Living Arts Center, Dayton, Ohio." EDUCATIONAL LEADERSHIP 27:191, 193, November, 1969.

Smith, E. E. "Wit, Creativity and Sarcasm" (bibliography). JOURNAL OF APPLIED PSYCHOLOGY 49:131-134, April, 1965.

Solomon, E. L. "Experience in Group Discussion." HIGH POINTS pp. 3-5, Spring, 1969.

Straus, M. S. "Communication Creativity and Problem-Solving Ability of Middle-and Working-Class Families in 3 Societies." AMERICAN JOURNAL OF SOCIOLOGY 73:417-430, January, 1968.

The Communicative Arts

Strunk, B. B. "Programs in Progress: Sensitivity Training."
SCHOOL MANAGEMENT 13:58-60, September, 1969.

Tannenbaum, S. "Who Owns Creativity?" MEDIA-SCOPE 13:64-65,
May, 1969.

Taylor, J. W. "Now, About Old Dogs/New Tricks." PERSONNEL
JOURNAL 47:786, November, 1968.

"Test Your Creativity." NATIONS BUSINESS 53:80-83, June, 1965.

Thomas, D. and T. Smith. "T-Grouping: The White Collar Hippie
Movement." NATIONAL ASSOCIATION OF SECONDARY-
SCHOOL PRINCIPALS BULLETIN 52:109, February, 1968.

Thomas, E. Llewellyn. "Movements of the Eye." SCIENTIFIC
AMERICAN 219:88-95, August, 1968.

Tinker, J. "Today's Creative Man, Cog or Wheel?" TELEVISION
17:38-41, February, 1960.

Torrance, E. P. "Creative Positives of Disadvantaged Children and
Youth" (bibliography). GIFTED CHILD QUARTERLY 13:71-81,
Summer, 1969.

"Touch-Touch Creativity: What A Psychologist Says." MARKETING/
COMMUNICATIONS 297:34, February, 1969.

Volckhause, G. "Some Tips on Improving Your Idea Creativity."
BURROUGHS CLEARING HOUSE 51:36, March, 1967.

Wallace, W. H. "Some Dimensions of Creativity." PERSONNEL
JOURNAL 46:363-370, 438-443, 458, June-July-August, 1967.

Wallen, N. E. "Creativity--Fantasy and Fact." EDUCATION
DIGEST 30:18-20, September, 1964.

Watson, E. R. "Group Communications and Developmental Processes" (bibliography). HIGH SCHOOL JOURNAL 52:431-440,

May, 1969.

Welden, T. A. "Small Group Applications of Q-Technique."
SPEECH MONOGRAPHS 36:68-72, March, 1969.

Wight, A. R. "What Does an Organization want: Creativity?"
ADULT LEADERSHIP 13:200-202, January, 1965.

Williams, F. E. "New Perspective on Creativity." PERSONNEL
ADMINISTRATION 29:3-5, July, 1966.

Winkler, R. "Creativity; How Did It All Begin?" PRINTERS INK
266:68, January 16, 1959.

Wolf, H. R. "Composition and Group Dynamics: The Paradox of
Freedom." COLLEGE ENGLISH 30:441-444, March, 1969.

Wood, R. V. and A. A. Goldberg. "Effects of 3 Styles of Training
Upon Small Group Effectiveness; Traditional, T-Group and In-
strumental Training Styles" (bibliography). SPEECH TEACHER
17:238-245, September, 1968.

Yamamoto, K. " 'Creativity'--a Blind Man's Report On the Ele-
phant" (bibliography). JOURNAL OF COUNSELLING PSYCHOL-
OGY 12,4:428-434, 1965.

BOOKS

Allen, V. L. "Situational Factors in Conformity." in L.
Berkowitz, ed. ADVANCES IN EXPERIMENTAL SOCIAL
PSYCHOLOGY, Vol. 2. New York: Academic Press, 1965,
pp. 133-175.

Beal, George M. LEADERSHIP AND DYNAMIC GROUP ACTION.

Ames, Iowa: Iowa State University Press, 1962.

Cartwright, D. and A. Zander, eds. GROUP DYNAMICS. New York: Harper and Row, 1968.

Collins, B. E. and B. H. Raven. "Group Structure: Attraction, Coalitions, Communication, and Power." in G. Lindzey and E. Aronson, eds. THE HANDBOOK OF SOCIAL PSYCHOLOGY, Vol. 4. Reading, Massachusetts: Addison Wesley, 1969, pp. 102-204.

Feather, N. T. "A Structural Balance Approach to the Analysis of Communication Effects." in L. Berkowitz, ed. ADVANCES IN EXPERIMENTAL SOCIAL PSYCHOLOGY, Vol. 3. New York: Academic Press, 1967, pp. 100-165.

Golembiewski, R. T. and A. Blumberg, eds. SENSITIVITY TRAINING AND THE LABORATORY APPROACH: READINGS ABOUT CONCEPTS AND APPLICATIONS. Itasca, Illinois: Beacock Publishers, 1970.

Hammesfahr, James E. CREATIVE GLASS BLOWING. San Francisco: Freeman and Company, 1968.

Hoffman, L. R. "Group Problem Solving." in L. Berkowitz, ed. ADVANCES IN EXPERIMENTAL SOCIAL PSYCHOLOGY, Vol. 2. New York: Academic Press, 1965, pp. 99-132.

Hollander, E. P. and J. W. Julian. "Studies in Leader Legitimacy, Influence, and Innovation." in L. Berkowitz, ed. ADVANCES IN EXPERIMENTAL SOCIAL PSYCHOLOGY, Vol. 5. New York: Academic Press, 1970, pp. 34-69.

Jones, E. E. and H. B. Gerard. FOUNDATIONS OF SOCIAL PSYCHOLOGY. New York: Wiley, 1967, pp. 331-386.

Kelley, H. H. and J. W. Thibaut. "Group Problem Solving." in G. Lindzey and E. Aronson, eds. THE HANDBOOK OF SOCIAL PSYCHOLOGY, Vol. 4. Reading, Massachusetts: Addison

Wesley, 1969, pp. 1-101.

Lakin, M. INTERPERSONAL ENCOUNTER: THEORY AND PRACTICE IN SENSITIVITY TRAINING. New York: McGraw Hill, 1972.

Morton, Jack Andrew. ORGANIZING FOR INNOVATION. New York: McGraw-Hill, 1971.

Nobel Conference, 6th. Gustavus Adolphus College, 1970. CREATIVITY; A DISCUSSION AT THE NOBEL CONFERENCE.... ST. PETER, MINNESOTA. New York: Fleet Academic Editions, 1970.

Olmsted, Donald W. SOCIAL GROUPS, ROLES AND LEADERSHIP: AN INTRODUCTION TO THE CONCEPTS. East Lansing: Michigan State University, 1961.

Petrullo, Luigi and Bernard M. Bass, eds. LEADERSHIP AND INTERPERSONAL BEHAVIOR. Englewood Cliffs, New Jersey: Prentice-Hall, 1961.

Phillips, Gerald M. COMMUNICATION AND THE SMALL GROUP. New York: Bobbs-Merrill, 1966.

Rogers, Carl Ransom. CARL ROGERS ON ENCOUNTER GROUPS. 1st ed. New York: Harper and Row, 1970.

Shaw, M. E. "Communication Networks." in L. Berkowitz, ed. ADVANCES IN EXPERIMENTAL SOCIAL PSYCHOLOGY, Vol 1. New York: Academic Press, 1964, pp. 111-147.

Sherif, M. SOCIAL INTERACTION: PROCESS AND PRODUCTS. Chicago: Aldine, 1967.

Smith, H. C. SENSITIVITY TO PEOPLE. New York: McGraw-Hill, 1966.

Taylor, C. W. "Some Possible Relations Between Communication

Abilities and Creative Abilities.'' in C. W. Taylor and F. Barron, eds. SCIENTIFIC CREATIVITY: ITS RECOGNITION AND DEVEL-OPMENT. New York: Wiley, 1963, pp. 365-371.

CREATIVITY IN MASS MEDIA

(RADIO, TV, JOURNALISM)

PERIODICALS

"Aerospace Television and Surveyor." SOCIETY OF MOTION
PICTURE & TELEVISION ENGINEERS JOURNAL 77:299-353,
April, 1968.

Bagdikion, Ben H. "Journalism's Wholesalers: a Golden Age of
Oracles; How Editors Pick Columnists; the Columnist as Prophet;
the Way It Was and the Way I Call Them; an Appraisal of the
Accuracy of Public Affairs Columnists; Oracles & Their Audiences." COLUMBIA JOURNALISM REVIEW 4:27-33, Fall, 1965;
4:11-16, Winter, 1966; 5:40-45, Spring, 1966; 5:35-39, Summer,
1966; 5:5-10, Fall, 1966; 5:22-29, Winter, 1966-1967.

Beck, L. F. "Strange World of Dr. Beck." AUDIOVISUAL IN-
STRUCTION 9:388-389, September, 1964.

"Bird of the Iron Feather." CHICAGO TRIBUNE Sec. 1A, p. 11,
January 19, 1970.

Bishop, Jerry E. "Tomorrow's Television: Engineers Say Shows
May Be Sent Directly From Satellite to Home...." WALL STREET
JOURNAL 168:1, September 26, 1966.

Blackburn, T. E. "Marquette Experiments With Closed Circuit
TV." CATHOLIC SCHOOL JOURNAL 63:54-56, May, 1963.

Bland, T. A. "Last Prom; One of the Most Stirring Traffic Safety
Documentaries Ever Created." SAFETY EDUCATION 43:2-7,
April, 1964.

The Communicative Arts

Blank, D. M. "Quest for Quantity and Diversity in Television Programming." AMERICAN ECONOMIC REVIEW PAPERS & PROCEEDINGS 56:467-475, May, 1966.

Blundell, William E. "Vying for Viewers: UHF TV Stations Aim Programs at Audiences with Special Interests." WALL STREET JOURNAL 165:1, February 19, 1965.

Boodish, H. M. "Crisis in American Education; Comments & Reflections on a TV Program, 'The Great Challenge'." SOCIAL STUDIES 54:183-187, October, 1963.

Brown, Stanley H. "Hollywood Rides Again (Deals That Give Networks' Rights to Screen Recent Movie Features)." FORTUNE 74:181-182, November, 1966.

Byerly, Kenneth R. "Newspaper Battle in Suburbia: Goliath vs. David: the Once-lowly Community Newspaper Has Overtaken the Giant Metropolitan Dailies in the Suburbs." MEDIA-SCOPE 8:58-60, August, 1964.

Clark, Monroe. "Cinerama, Inc's New Dimension; Under New Management Since January 1960, the Specialty Movie Maker Has Diversified Into the OPTICAL SCIENCE Field and Further Developed Its Own Stature in the Entertainment Area." FINANCE 81:33-34, November 15, 1963.

"Closed Circuit Experiment; Village College TV." TIMES EDUCATIONAL SUPPLEMENT 2484:842, December 28, 1962.

Coon, Thomas F. "Free Press Need Not Be Trial by Newspaper." POLICE 12:41-44, March-April, 1968.

"Creativity in Industrial Advertising and Marketing." PRINTERS' INK 281:24-27, December 21, 1962.

Daniels, Draper. "Creativity Molds Its Personality." PRINTERS' INK 283:155-158, May 29, 1964.

Dodd, Allen R. "Is TV Really Too Commercial? Opinions of Men in Advertising, Broadcasting and Government Who Deal With This Problem Every Day; Programming: The Great TV Debate." PRINTERS' INK 278:21, 25-27, February 9, 1962.

Dreyfus, L. S. "Enrichment Through Radio & Television." NATIONAL ASSOCIATION OF SECONDARY-SCHOOL PRINCI-PALS BULLETIN 50:111-115, October, 1966.

Edelstein, Alex S. and J. Blaine Schultz. "The Weekly News-paper's Leadership Role As Seen By Community Leaders...." JOURNALISM QUARTERLY 40:565-574, Autumn, 1963.

"Erratic Winds of Change: American Educational Publishers In-stitute's National Education Association's Joint Dilemma." PUBLISHER'S WEEKLY 196:31-32, December 26, 1969.

Evans, F. L. "Safety Story Lady Makes TV Debut." SAFETY EDU-CATION 41:12-13, March, 1962.

"Experimental Series of Lectures for Teachers Utilizes the Com-puter, Television, and the Telephone." IEEE SPECTRUM 5:125, March, 1968.

Farr, K. E. "Phonovid, a System for Recording Television Pictures on Phonograph Records." AUDIO ENGINEERING SOCIETY JOURNAL 16:163-167, April, 1968.

Freniere, E. A. "Through a Glass Eye Brightly." JOURNAL OF GENERAL EDUCATION 12:235-238, October, 1959.

Garnder, Martin. "Mathematical Games." SCIENTIFIC AMERICAN 219:140, November, 1968.

Gibson, James W. "Creativity in the Speech Classroom." CENTRAL STATES SPEECH JOURNAL 15:129-133, May, 1964.

Gillion, M. E. "Making History Live; Studying Yellow Journalism." CALIFORNIA TEACHERS ASSOCIATION JOURNAL 60:30-32,

January, 1964.

"Great Adventure; a Landmark in TV Drama." ARIZONA TEACHER 52:17, September, 1963.

Grubb, C. Norton. "Newspaper Industry in Significant Era of Change." PRINTING AND PUBLISHING 8:6-8, July, 1967.

Harrell, J. G. "Inescapable Impact of Mass Media." INTERNATIONAL JOURNAL OF RELIGIOUS EDUCATION 40:6-9, February, 1964.

Hickey, Neil and Susan Ludel. "Is TV Looking At Russia Through Red-Colored Glasses? Soviet Censorship, Some Experts Charge, Makes It Difficult For Documentaries To See the Blemishes On the Face of the USSR; How the Soviets Keep Control Over What Can Be Filmed." TV GUIDE 15:6-11, August 5, 1967; 15:19-23, August 12, 1967.

"High School Independent Press Service, New York. H.S. Underground Press Editorial." RESEARCH REPORTS p. 639, August 27, 1969.

Hilliard, R. L. "New Directions in Educational Broadcasting." AUDIOVISUAL INSTRUCTION 11:13-15, January, 1966.

Hoff, D. C. "Med-aid; an Amateur Radio Service." QST 51:56-57, November, 1967.

Hope, F. "Nude Steak Behind Gause." NEW STATESMAN 76:58, July 12, 1968.

Houlton, Robert. "The Process of Innovation: Magnetic Recording and the Broadcasting Industry in the USA." OXFORD UNIVERSITY INSTITUTE OF ECONOMICS AND STATISTICS BULLETIN 29: 41-59, February, 1967.

"How Radio is Flexible as an Advertising Medium." MEDIA-SCOPE 7:69-72, August, 1963; 7:74, September, 1963; 7:76, October, 1963.

"Irrigating the Wasteland." ECONOMIST 225:627-628, November 11, 1967.

"The Irrepressible Weeklies: INNER CITY VOICE (Detroit), by LaRue Heard; the PITTSBURGH POINT, by James A. Grossman; The INTERMOUNTAIN OBSERVER (Idaho), by John Stevens and Bert Cross; The CHAPEL HILL (North Carolina) WEEKLY, by Roger M. Williams." COLUMBIA JOURNALISM REVIEW 7:30-40, Summer, 1968.

Isaacs, J. "Future of Television Journalism." ENCOUNTER 30: 84-90, March, 1968.

Jorgensen, E. "Night Call." AUDIOVISUAL INSTRUCTION 14:55, June, 1969.

Kappel, Frederick R. "TV Gets a Boost Through Space: AT & T's Telstar Satellite Opens New Era Of World Wide Communications with First Live Trans-Atlantic TV Broadcast...." BUSINESS WEEK pp. 32-33, July 14, 1962.

Keithahn, M. N. "Teen Age Problem On The Air." JOURNAL OF RELIGIOUS EDUCATION 42:6-7, July, 1966.

Kraus, S. "Modifying Prejudice: Attitude Change as a Function of the Race of the Communicator" (bibliography). AUDIOVISUAL COMMUNICATIONS REVIEW 10:14-22, January, 1962.

Lamb, H. W. Jr. "WRHS: Growing Into Educational Broadcasting; Robbinsville, N. C." EDUCATIONAL SCREEN AND AUDIO-VISUAL GUIDE 47:12-13, December, 1968.

Levitt, Theodore. "Creativity is Not Enough (Importance of Proper Implementation Of Ideas)." HARVARD BUSINESS REVIEW 41:72-83, May-June, 1963.

"Live TV Leaps the Ocean: U.S., Europe Swap Telstar Broadcasts, But Regular Transmission Is a Long Way Off." BUSINESS WEEK pp. 28-29, July 28, 1962.

The Communicative Arts

McCombs, Maxwell E. "Negro Use of Television and Newspapers
    For Political Information, 1952-64." JOURNAL OF BROAD-
    CASTING 12:261-266, Summer, 1968.

McKown, V. "WNAS; Innovative Actions by Creative Youngsters
    for Alert Educators." AUDIOVISUAL INSTRUCTION 12:152-153,
    February, 1967.

"Man, Beast and The Land; Gas Industry's Documentary On
    Africa." AMERICAN GAS ASSOCIATION MONTHLY 50:12-13,
    April, 1968.

Maneloveg, H. "Media Choice May Be More Creative Than The
    Message." ADVERTISING AGE 39:60, February 5, 1968.

Maxwell, M. G. "Cameras That Wink Can Produce 3-d TV."
    ELECTRONICS 41:132-133, March 18, 1968.

Merrill, John. "Global Patterns of Elite Daily Journalism."
    JOURNALISM QUARTERLY 45:99-105, Spring, 1968.

Merrill, John C. "Panel Names World's Ten Leading 'Quality'
    Dailies; a Panel of 26 International Communications Professors
    Picks a 'Top 20' World Newspapers and Ranks Top 10."
    JOURNALISM QUARTERLY 41:568-572, Autumn, 1964.

Methvin, Eugene H. "Mass Media and Mass Violence." NEW
    LEADER 51:6-8, January 15, 1968.

Montagnon, P. "TV's Contribution to Open University." TIMES
    EDUCATIONAL SUPPLEMENT 2826:34, July 18, 1969.

Moyers, Bill. "Mass Media In the Age of Dissent." NEW LEADER
    51:10-13, November 18, 1969.

Nelson, G. V. "Instant TV Replay In the Lecture Hall."
    JOURNAL OF CHEMICAL EDUCATION 46:620, September,
    1969.

"Networks Take Cue From Stage '67: American Broadcasting
Company's Partial Success With a Cultural TV Series Has
Attracted Wide Interest, Encouraging the Other Networks To
Begin Some Experimenting on Their Own." BUSINESS WEEK
pp. 60-62, February 25, 1967.

Niefeld, Jaye S. "The Future of Spot Radio Sales." MEDIA-SCOPE
5:72, November, 1961.

Pack, R. "TV, a New World of Music for Children." MUSIC
JOURNAL 21:42, October, 1963.

Palmer, E. L. "Can Television Really Teach? Preschoolers
Watch Sesame Street Series." AMERICAN EDUCATION 5:2-6,
August, 1969.

Paltridge, J. G. "How To Plan Where and When to Use TV: After
Pinpointing Large Enrollment, Multiclass, Repetitively Taught
Classes, The U. of California Found That by Applying Television
In Only 5% Of Its Courses, It Could Serve Nearly 30% Of Its
Class Enrollments." COLLEGE AND UNIVERSITY BUSINESS
38:43-45, February, 1965.

Parkings, G. "KNXT Films 2 One-Hour Documentaries on Location
in Washington D.C." SCHOOL ACTIVITIES 34:45-46, October,
1962.

Parnes, Sidney J. "Can Creativity be Increased? Specialized Education Measurably Improves Creativity in Problem Solving."
PERSONNEL ADMINISTRATION 25:2-9, November-December,
1962.

Porter, P. "Words and Music." NEW STATESMAN 77:93,
January 17, 1969.

Potter, Joseph C. "What's Wrong With Hollywood? It Must Give
Greater Scope to Creative Producers, Writers and Artists Like
Those Responsible For the Success Of the Italian and French
Film Industries." CHALLENGE 12:35-37, January, 1964.

Prentice, M. "And the Screen Was Black." AUDIOVISUAL IN-STRUCTION 13:957-960, November, 1968.

"Professor Stars in Astronomy Over Four-city Video Circuit." PHYSICS TODAY 21:69, February, 1968.

"Remember Mr. Novak? Meet Mr. Dixon In Room 222!" TODAY'S EDUCATION 58:21, October, 1969.

Remley, F. M. "TV Playback on Tape and Film." OVERVIEW 2:48-49, December, 1961.

Riggs, Frank L. "The Changing Role of Radio: Changes in Radio Programming, Audiences and Effects in the United States... Trends Today." JOURNAL OF BROADCASTING 8:331-339, Fall, 1964.

Robertson, R. N. "Utility Uses Educational TV To Tell Electric Cooking Story." ELECTRONICS WORLD 168:43, October 30, 1967.

Rose, Harold. "How Much Is a Piece Of Film? Cinema Is One of the Most Potent Forms of Communication, Yet Many Firms Have Not Yet Realized All the Possibilities of the Industrial Film." WESTMINSTER REVIEW pp. 8-12, February, 1963.

Rowland, H. S. "Journalism vs. The Mass Media, Unit On Radio and Television News Reporting." ENGLISH JOURNAL 53:345-348, May, 1964.

Rowley, P. "Serious U.S. TV Fights For Life." NEW STATESMAN 77:500-501, April 11, 1969.

Russo, F. "BBC, Sex and 1986." ATLAS pp. 48-49, November, 1968.

Saneholtz, B. J. "ITV Cries For the Creative Approach." JOURNAL OF HOME ECONOMICS 56:329-331, May, 1964.

Saunders, D. C. "Ham School In the Blue Ridge Mountains." QST 51:53-54, November, 1967.

"Sesame Street." PUBLISHERS WEEKLY 197:31, January 12, 1970.

Shanley, John P. "Television's Time of Decision: Flying Class-rooms and Pay TV Promise Some Relief From Gunshots and Talking Horses." COUNTRY BEAUTIFUL 1:34-41, February, 1962.

Smith, A. "Radio: Steppingstone in Speech." TEXAS OUTLOOK 46:28-29, February, 1962.

"Spreading a Net for Hijackers: a Radio-controlled Systems Tying Truckers Together Is Helping Cut Thefts of Trucks, Cargoes." BUSINESS WEEK pp. 171-172, May 6, 1967.

Stevenson, Robert L. "Readability of Conservative and Sensa-tional Papers Since 1872: Six U. S. Dailies." JOURNALISM QUARTERLY 41:210-216, Spring, 1964.

Stocker, J. "Mr. Novak; a New and Different TV Series." ARIZONA TEACHER 52:16-17, September, 1963.

Stone, Richard. " 'Hip' Papers: The Underground Press Succeeds by Intriguing Rebels and 'Squares'." WALL STREET JOURNAL 171:1, March 4, 1968.

Stretch, B. B. "Sesame Street Opens." SATURDAY REVIEW OF LITERATURE 52:91, November 15, 1969.

Stroh, N. K. "How a Diary Encouraged Creative Writing." ELEMEN-TARY ENGLISH 46:769-771, October, 1969.

Stuart, Frederic. "Brighter Prospects For Color TV: Story of an Innovation." CHALLENGE 9:31-34, April, 1961.

"Telstar's TV Future Is Foggy; Time Zone Differences and Cost May Limit TV Networks' Use of AT & TIs Communications

Satellite...." BUSINESS WEEK pp. 32-33, July 21, 1962.

"The 'Television Fiasco'; Interview with Fred W. Friendly, TV Authority." U. S. NEWS 62:58-62, June 12, 1967.

"Tracking Ships To Use Lasers For Accuracy." AEROSPACE TECHNOLOGY 21:54, November 6, 1967.

"Tune In On Censorship; SAM BENEDICT Show and DEFENDERS." WILSON LIBRARY BULLETIN 37:724, May, 1963.

Turnstile, N. B. "Air (Proposals For The University of the Air)." NEW STATESMAN 71:326, March 11, 1966.

"TV and Hollywood Play a New Duet...Movie made for TV...." BUSINESS WEEK pp. 107-108, April 16, 1966.

Unruh, G. G. "Television; a Tool for Innovation." SPECTRUM 45:16-17, May, 1969.

Van Hadley, Harlan. "H. E. L. P. for Motorists (Use of Highway Emergency Locating Plan, Calling for Use of Citizen's Band, Two-way Radio Equipment In Private Passenger Cars)." ASSOCIATION MANAGEMENT 17:26-28, July, 1965.

Weitzner, Jay. "The Neglected Media; Television and Radio Offer Opportunities That Are Often Missed by Print-oriented Publicists." PUBLIC RELATIONS JOURNAL 24:20, November, 1968.

Wetmore, W. C. "Airborne TV Studied by Emerging Nations." AVIATION WEEK 88:37, January 8, 1968.

White, H. F. "Put Creativity Into Press Functions; Specialties Can Add Impact and Favorable Idea Retention." PUBLIC RELATIONS JOURNAL 24:37-38, February, 1968.

White, J. F. "Communications for What?" ADULT LEADERSHIP 12:224-226, February, 1964.

Woods, W. K. "I'll Trade You 10 George Hamilton's For One Sky Diving Grandmother." NORTH AMERICAN REVIEW 5:39, May, 1968.

Worsnop, Richard L. "Competing Media." EDITORIAL RESEARCH REPORTS 11,3:531, July 18, 1969.

Wren, G. S. "TV's Misterogers: Quality Clicks With Kids." LOOK 33:102-106, December 2, 1969.

Wright, Charles R. "Television and Radio Program Ratings and Measurements: a Selected and Annotated Bibliography." JOURNAL OF BROADCASTING 5:165-186, Spring, 1961.

BOOKS

Agee, Warren. MASS MEDIA IN A FREE SOCIETY. Lawrence, Kansas: University of Kansas Press, 1969.

Beal, George M. LEADERSHIP AND DYNAMIC GROUP ACTION. Ames, Iowa: Iowa State University Press, 1962.

Bradley, Duane. THE NEWSPAPER--ITS PLACE IN A DEMOCRACY. New York: Van Nostrand, 1965.

Casty, Alan, ed. MASS MEDIA AND MASS MAN. New York: Holt, Rinehart and Winston, 1968.

Fabun, Don. COMMUNICATIONS: THE TRANSFER OF MEANING. Beverly Hills: Glencoe Press, 1968.

Hazard, Patrick D., ed. TV AS ART: SOME ESSAYS IN CRITICISM. National Council Of Teachers Of English, 1966.

Lent, John S. NEWHOUSE, NEWSPAPERS, NUISANCES: HIGH-LIGHTS IN THE GROWTH OF A COMMUNICATIONS EMPIRE. Jerico, New York: Exposition Press, 1966.

McLuhan, Herbert Marshall and Quentin Piore. THE MEDIUM IS THE MESSAGE. New York: Bantam Books, 1967.

McLuhan, Herbert Marshall. UNDERSTANDING THE MEDIA: THE EXTENSIONS OF MAN. New York: Signet Books, 1964.

Olmsted, Donald W. SOCIAL GROUPS, ROLES AND LEADERSHIP: AN INTRODUCTION TO THE CONCEPTS. Institute of Community Development, Continuing Education Service. East Lansing: Michigan State University, 1961.

Petrullo, Luigi and Bernard M. Bass, eds. LEADERSHIP AND INTERPERSONAL BEHAVIOR. Englewood Cliffs, New Jersey: Prentice-Hall, 1961.

Sohn, David A. THE CREATIVE EYE. Dayton, Ohio: Pflaum, 1970.

Weiss, W. "Effects of the Mass Media of Communication." in G. Lindzey and E. Aronson, eds. THE HANDBOOK OF SOCIAL PSYCHOLOGY, Vol. V. Reading, Massachusetts: Addison Wesley, 1969, pp. 77-195.

Wiseman, T. Jan and Molly J. Wiseman. CREATIVE COMMUNICA-TIONS: TEACHING MASS MEDIA. Minneapolis: National Scholastic Press Association, 1971.

CREATIVITY IN MUSIC

PERIODICALS

"Adventure in Sound--Syn-Ket." TIME 91:79, May 24, 1968.

Alper, Herbert. "The Bennington Approach to Creative Learning."
    MUSIC EDUCATORS' JOURNAL 49,5:41-43, April-May, 1963.

Ames, Morgan. "Tom Swift and His Electric Everything." HIGH
    FIDELITY INCORPORATING MUSICAL AMERICA 18:46,
    March, 1968.

Baldus, Sister Joseph Mary. "The Dynamics of Creativity." MUSIC
    JOURNAL 27:94-95, April, 1969.

Barbour, Richard Lee. "A Study of Perceptions of Selected Innova-
    tive Statements in Music Education by Principals and Music Teach-
    ers in Oregon Secondary Schools." DISSERTATION ABSTRACTS
    30,4 Sec. A:1584-A, October, 1969.

Bar-Illan, David. "Drop-in Night at the Electric Circus." SATURDAY
    REVIEW 52:72-73, November 15, 1969.

Barnum, Walter. "Music for the Talented: A Program in Action."
    MUSIC EDUCATORS' JOURNAL 47,5:37-40, April-May, 1961.

Bergan, John R. "Pitch, Perception, Imagery, and Regression in
    the Service of the Ego." JOURNAL OF RESEARCH IN MUSIC
    EDUCATION 13,1:15-32, Spring, 1965.

Berger, Donald P. "Creative Music Education." MUSIC EDUCATORS'

The Communicative Arts

JOURNAL 50,2:79-81, November-December, 1963.

Berger, Ivan. "Adventures with a Musical Erector Set; the Putney Synthesizer." SATURDAY REVIEW 53:40-41, December 26, 1970.

---. "Switched on Bach." SATURDAY REVIEW 52:45-57, 59, January 25, 1969.

Berkovitz, Robert. "The Future of Music in Perspective, Being a Report on the Entropic Synthesizer or After Moog What?" AMERICAN RECORD GUIDE 35:180-182, November, 1968.

Bernheimer, Martin. "Musical Past and the Electronic Future." SATURDAY REVIEW 47:63-65, October 31, 1964; pp. 65-66, November 28, 1964.

Boretz, Benjamin. "Music Avoidance of Recent Works." NATION 194:522-524, June 9, 1962.

---. "New Music and the American Mainstream." NATION 198:466-468, May 4, 1964.

Bowers, Faubion. "Feast of Astonishments Festival of the Avant-Garde." NATION 199:172-175, September 28, 1964.

Brown, Elwood Hansel. "A Study of the Application of Creativity in the Teaching of Secondary School Music." DISSERTATION ABSTRACTS 29,5 Sec. A:1553-A, November, 1968.

Burgstahler, E. E. "Factors Influencing the Choice and Pursuance of a Career in Music Education: A Survey and Case Study Approach." MISSOURI JOURNAL OF RESEARCH IN MUSIC EDUCATION 2:53-57, 1967.

"Business of Culture; Symposium." SATURDAY REVIEW 53:17-32, February 28, 1970.

"Can Creative Awards Be Dangerous?" MUSICAL AMERICA 80:8, June, 1960.

Canfield, Susan T. "Creativity in Music Education." MUSIC EDUCA-
TORS' JOURNAL 48,2:51-56, November-December, 1961.

Carey, Margaretta. "Music for the Educable Mentally Retarded."
MUSIC EDUCATORS' JOURNAL 46,4:72-74, February-March, 1960.

Castaldo, Joseph. "Creativity Can End Our Musical Isolation."
MUSIC EDUCATORS' JOURNAL 56:36-38, November, 1969.

Christopher, Sister Mary Eunice. "Music Education in Tomorrow's
Schools." MUSART 21,6:34-35, 1969.

"Color of Sound." NEW YORKER 43:25 26, February 17, 1968.

"Composer Uses Printing Press for Inspiration." PUBLISHERS'
WEEKLY 191:116-117, March 6, 1967.

"Composing by Knucklebone; Aleatoric Music." TIME 79:55-56,
April 13, 1962.

"Conforming with the Avant-Garde." HARPER 238:112,114, April,
1969.

Cunningham, Eloise. "Osaka; Eclectic Native Opera." MUSICAL
AMERICA 80:9, June, 1960.

Daniel, Oliver. "Anarchy and Order: Dockstader's Eight Electronic
Pieces." SATURDAY REVIEW 46:73, October 26, 1963.

Danziger, Harris. "Our Teachers May Be in Another World."
MUSIC EDUCATORS' JOURNAL 56:25-59, October, 1969.

Dickinson, P. "Composing at School." MUSIC IN EDUCATION
29,315:222, 1965.

"Does Anybody Need the Avant-Garde?" HARPER 232:108-110,
June, 1966.

"Does Musical Education Give Encouragement to Initiative and

Originality?'' MUSIC & DANCE 54:17-18, July, 1963.

Earle, Anitra. ''Center for Contemporary Music: Mills College, Oakland, California.'' HIGH FIDELITY/MUSICAL AMERICA 20:24-25, September, 1970, MA.

Ehle, Robert C. ''Make Your Own Electronic Music.'' RADIO-ELECTRONICS 40:52, May, 1969.

---. ''Plain and Easy Guide to Practical Electronic Music.'' HIGH FIDELITY 19:50-56, August, 1969.

''Electronic Rock: The United States of America Appearance at Judson Hall.'' NEW YORKER 44:29, March 30, 1968.

Evett, Robert. ''Dial It Yourself.'' NEW REPUBLIC 156:33-35, April 15, 1967.

''Far-out at the Philharmonic; Bangs and Gurgles.'' TIME 83:79, February 14, 1964.

''Father; Music Without Instruments or Electronic Music.'' NEW YORKER 39:25, January 18, 1964.

Fitzgerald, R. B. ''Creative Music Teaching in the Elementary School.'' NEA JOURNAL 53:42-43, December, 1964.

''For Aleatoric Ears; New York's Premiere of Larry Austin's Improvisations....'' NEWSWEEK 63:80, January 20, 1964.

Foss, Lukas. ''Composition in the 1960's .'' HIGH FIDELITY INCORPORATING MUSICAL AMERICA 18:42, September, 1968.

---. ''Improvisation vs. Composition.'' MUSICAL AMERICA 82:48, May, 1962.

Foster, Donald L. ''Can Creativity Be Taught?'' MUSIC JOURNAL 27:36, 38, March, 1969.

Fowler, Charles B. "Discovery Method, Its Relevance for Music Education." JOURNAL OF RESEARCH IN MUSIC EDUCATION 14,2:126-134, Summer, 1966.

Fried, Irving M. "The Prospects for Psychoacoustics." HIGH FIDELITY INCORPORATING MUSICAL AMERICA 13:48-50, 116, April, 1963.

Frisch, Bruce H. "This Man is Composing Music in the Strange New Field of Electronic Music." SCIENCE DIGEST 57:72-75, February, 1965.

Fuller, Richard Buckminster. "The Music of the New Life; Thoughts on Creativity, Sensorial Reality, and Comprehensiveness." MUSIC EDUCATORS' JOURNAL 52,5 & 6:46-48, 124-146, April-May, 1966; pp. 52-68, June-July, 1966.

Gerstel, Judith. "Major Musical Precedent; Totally Subsidized by Government." HIGH FIDELITY 20 Sec. 2:25, August, 1970.

Giles, Allen and Robert Ricci. "An Experimental Music Curriculum for Gifted High School Students." MUSIC EDUCATORS' JOURNAL 53,3:57-60, November, 1966.

Glanville-Hicks, Peggy. "Music; How It's Built." VOGUE 147:200, March 1, 1966.

"Guggenheim Roulette; Aleatoric Music." REPORTER 26:35-37, January 4, 1962.

Hamilton, David. "Music: Crisis of Confidence in the Future of Serious Music." NATION 210:317-318, March 16, 1970.

Hanson, Howard. "Cultivating a Climate for Creativity." MUSIC EDUCATORS' JOURNAL 46,6:28-30, June-July, 1960.

Herman, Carter. "How Electronic Music Got That Way." ATLANTIC 222:138, 140, 143, December, 1968.

---. "Revolt of the Composers." ATLANTIC 222:129-132, September, 1968.

Hartung, Ernest W. "The Place of the Artist in Contemporary Society." MUSIC EDUCATORS' JOURNAL 55:77-78, 81-82, September, 1968.

Hausamman, Suzanne. "Sound of Music Etched in Light." LIFE 50:58-63, May 26, 1961.

Herbert, Clarke L. "They Shall Have Music." AMERICAN EDUCATION 2:22, October, 1966.

Hiemenz, J. "Moog at the Museum." HIGH FIDELITY INCORPORATING MUSICAL AMERICA 19:20-21, November, 1969, MA.

Hiller, Lejaren and James Beauchamp. "Research in Music with Electronics." SCIENCE 150:161-169, October 8, 1965.

Holderried, Elizabeth S. "Creativity in My Classroom." MUSIC EDUCATORS' JOURNAL 55:37-39, March, 1969.

"Into Our Lives With Moog." TIME 93:50-51, March 7, 1969.

"Is It Music? Disciples of John Cage." NEWSWEEK 62:53, September 2, 1963.

Ivey, Donald. "An Eclectic Concept of Music Humanities." MUSIC EDUCATORS' JOURNAL 51,6:34-38, June-July, 1965.

Jacobson, Bernard. "In Composers." HIGH FIDELITY 19:54-57, July, 1969.

Jenkins, Speight, Jr. "Bright Future? A Self-Appointed Seer Argues for Color and Super-Realism to Sell Wagner." OPERA NEWS 33:8-12, February 22, 1969.

Jenny, Hans. "Music Made Visible in a Film of Liquid Cymatics." UNESCO COURIER 22:10-12, 16, 18, 29-30, December, 1969.

Jones, Edna Marie. "Discovering Values of Music Through Creative Experiences." MUSIC EDUCATORS' JOURNAL 49,4:71-72, February-March, 1963.

Jones, Robert W. "Contemporary Music Project; Its Pay Off." HIGH FIDELITY INCORPORATING MUSICAL AMERICA 19:10-11, November, 1969, MA.

Kivy, Peter. "Child Mozart as an Aesthetic Symbol." JOURNAL OF THE HISTORY OF IDEAS 28:249-258, April, 1967.

Kostelanetz, Richard. "Two Extremes of Avant-Garde Music." NEW YORK TIMES MAGAZINE pp. 34, 52, 54-55, 57, 59, 62, 64, January 15, 1967.

Kuhn, Wolfgang E. and Raynold L. Allvin. "Computer-Assisted Teaching: a New Approach to Research in Music." COUNCIL FOR RESEARCH IN MUSIC EDUCATION BULLETIN 11:1-13, Fall, 1967.

Lamb, Hubert. "Music in the Age of Zak." HARPER 226:76-78, May, 1963.

Landis, Beth McLellan. "Experiments in Creativity." MUSIC EDUCATORS' JOURNAL 54:41-42, May, 1968.

Langyel, Peter. "Future Dimensions of Music." UNESCO COURIER 15:12-13, November, 1962.

London, Sol J. "Origins of Psychoacoustics." HIGH FIDELITY INCORPORATING MUSICAL AMERICA 13:44-47, 117, April, 1963.

McCluskey, Sister Anne. "Fostering Creativity." CLAVIER 8,2: 44-45, February, 1969.

Mayer, Martin. "Prodigies." ESQUIRE 61:106-107, May, 1964.

Miller, Thomas W. "The Influence of Progressivism on Music

Education, 1917-1947.'' JOURNAL OF RESEARCH IN MUSIC EDUCATION 14,1:3-16, Spring, 1966.

Mohn, Norman Carroll. "The Inter-Personal Manifestations of Creativity." AMERICAN MUSIC TEACHER 18,3:32-33, 47, January, 1969.

"Moment Musical; Scores for Commercials." NEWSWEEK 70:106, November 27, 1967.

Moog, Robert A. "Electronic Music, Its Composition and Performance." ELECTRONICS WORLD 77:42-46, 84-85, February, 1967.

Moor, Paul. "Sinus Tones with Nuts and Bolts." HARPER 225: 49-50, October, 1962.

Morgan, Robert E. "More Avant-Rock in the Classroom." ENGLISH JOURNAL 58:1238-1240, November, 1969.

"Music Centres and the Talented Child." MAKING MUSIC 62:8-9, Autumn, 1966.

Neilson, James. "Educational Creativity and 'Title III'." MUSIC JOURNAL 24:40, 73, April, 1966.

"Newport Jazz Festival." COMMONWEALTH 72:393-396, August 5, 1960.

"Newport Jazz Festival." NEWSWEEK 56:80, July 11, 1960.

"Newport Jazz Festival." NEW YORKER 36:84, 86-88, July 16, 1960.

"Newport Jazz Festival." NEW YORKER 35:162-163, September 26, 1959.

"Newport Jazz Festival." TIME 76:47, July 18, 1960.

Orenstein, Arbie. "Maurice Ravel's Creative Process." MUSICAL QUARTERLY 53:467-481, October, 1967.

Osborne, Conrad L. "Quest for Verismo." HIGH FIDELITY
INCORPORATING MUSICAL AMERICA 12:51-52, 54, 146-147,
November, 1962.

Pearman, Martha. "Bringing Music to the Gifted Child." MUSIC
JOURNAL 18:54, 73, September, 1960.

Pirie, Peter J. "Fie Upon-Freud! Psychoanalysis and Composers."
HIGH FIDELITY INCORPORATING MUSICAL AMERICA 14:31,
July, 1964.

---. "Unfashionable Generation; Twentieth Century Music."
HIGH FIDELITY INCORPORATING MUSICAL AMERICA 16:59,
January, 1966.

Purcell, William L. "Birds in Music." AMERICAN RECORD GUIDE
28:616-621, April, 1962.

Reimer, Bennett. "Leonard Meyer's Theory of Value and Greatness
in Music." JOURNAL OF RESEARCH IN MUSIC EDUCATION
10,2:87-99, Fall, 1962.

Reynolds, George Earle. "Environmental Sources of Musical
Awakening in Pre-School Children." DISSERTATION ABSTRACTS
21:1214-1215, November, 1960.

Rich, Leslie. "Music for Non-Listening." HIGH FIDELITY INCOR-
PORATING MUSICAL AMERICA 15:34, November, 1965.

Rich, Maria F. "U. S. Opera Survey: The Multiest of Media."
OPERA NEWS 34:13-16, November 22, 1969.

Robertson, F. H. "Combining Visual and Tonal Art." MUSIC
JOURNAL 18:56, 91, March, 1960.

Rogers, Harold, David Hughes and others. "Music at Harvard
Yesterday and Today." MUSICAL AMERICA 83:6-9, June, 1963.

Rosenstone, Robert A. " 'The Times They Are A-Changin': The

Music of Protest." ANNALS OF THE AMERICAN ACADEMY OF POLITICAL AND SOCIAL SCIENCE 382:131-144, March, 1969.

Russcol, Herbert. "Music Since Hiroshima: The Electronic Age Begins." AMERICAN SCHOLAR 39:289-293, Spring, 1970.

Saal, Hubert. "Electric Bach." NEWSWEEK 73:90, February 3, 1969.

Salzman, Eric. "Music From the Electronic Universe." HIGH FIDELITY INCORPORATING MUSICAL AMERICA 14:54, August, 1964.

Samples, Robert E. "Kari's Handicap, the Impediment of Creativity." SATURDAY REVIEW 50:56-57, July 15, 1967; Discussion 50:51, 72, August 19, 1967.

Sander, Ellen. "Ultimate Pop Experience, Woodstock Music and Art Fair." SATURDAY REVIEW 52:59, 65-66, September 27, 1969.

Sargeant, Winthrop. "Atonal Music in Performances of Concert Opera Association." NEW YORKER 40:125-129, February 29, 1964.

---. "Concert of Anti-Teleological Music at Judson Hall." NEW YORKER 39:120-123, September 14, 1963.

---. "Musical Events; Technique of Musical Composition Over the Past Half Century." NEW YORKER 39:164-166, September 28, 1963.

Scarfe, N. V. "Creative Dimensions in Education." MUSIC EDUCATORS' JOURNAL 49,1:25-27, September-October, 1962.

Schonberg, H. C. "Music: Making a Choice." HARPER 240:132, 134, May, 1970.

Schwinger, Wolfram. "Germany/The Avant-Garde." MUSICAL AMERICA 84:78, December, 1964.

Music

Scoppa, Bud. "Discovery Through Rock." SCHOLASTIC TEACHER pp. 14-15, October 5, 1970.

"Seeing Sounds. Electronic Music at Expo '67." TIME 90:48, 50, October 6, 1967.

Simpson, Donald James. "The Effect of Selected Musical Studies on Growth in General Creative Potential." DISSERTATION AB-STRACTS 30,2 Sec. A:502-A, August, 1969.

Smith-Brindle, Reginald. "Serial Composition." MUSICAL QUART-ERLY 55:125-131, January, 1969.

"Sound of Cybernetics; Aleatory Music Performed by New York Philharmonic Orchestra." NEWSWEEK 63:88, February 17, 1964.

Steinberg, Michael. "Twelve-Tone for Everyman." SATURDAY REVIEW 44:39, May 27, 1961.

"Stimulant or Tranquilizer; Symposium." HOUSE AND GARDEN 136: 26, 28, 102, July, 1969.

"Stratford, Ont., Engineers Lead Composers." MUSICAL AMERICA 80:33, October, 1960.

"Swurpledeewurpledeezeech; Signature Music." TIME 88:68, November 4, 1966.

Thiel, Jorn. "Technical Media in the Academy of Music and the Creative Arts." MUSIC EDUCATORS' JOURNAL 47,6:59-64, June-July, 1961.

"Third Stream Music." NEW YORKER 37:42-44, December 9, 1961.

Thomas, Ronald B. "A Study of New Concepts, Procedures, and Achievements in Music Learning as Developed in Selected Music Education Programs." COUNCIL FOR RESEARCH IN MUSIC EDUCATION BULLETIN 6:25-26, Fall, 1965.

Thompson, E. D. "Do We Motivate Learning?" THE SCHOOL MUSICIAN 39:56-57, December, 1967.

Thomson, Virgil. "America's Musical Maturity, a Twentieth Century Story." YALE REVIEW 51:66-74, October, 1961.

Tolbert, Mary R. "Experimental Scheduling in Midwest Schools." MUSIC EDUCATORS' JOURNAL 52,1:69-72, 170-171, September-October, 1965.

Tomkins, Calvin. "Profiles; Avant-Garde Music of John Cage." NEW YORKER 40:64-68, 71-78, 80-88, 90-96, 99-106, 111-118, 121-128, November 28, 1964.

Turetzky, Bertram J. "Vocal and Speech Sounds--a Technique of Contemporary Writing for the Contrabass." THE COMPOSER (US) 1,3:118-119, 1969.

Turner, Joseph. "Innovation and Experiment in Music Education." COUNCIL FOR RESEARCH IN MUSIC EDUCATION BULLETIN 6:1-8, Fall, 1965.

Vauclain, Constant. "An Experiment in Musical Texture." MUSICAL QUARTERLY 51,2:318-335, April, 1965.

Velde, Paul. "Electronic Noel; Production by the Electric Circus, Inc., in Carnegie Hall." COMMONWEALTH 87:471-472, January 19, 1968.

Wallace, Kenneth Dean. "20th Century Innovations, More or Less." HIGH FIDELITY INCORPORATING MUSICAL AMERICA 16: 18-19, 30, October, 1966, MA.

Weinstein, Robert V. "Music Machines Replace Humans." MUSIC JOURNAL 27:38-39, September, 1969.

Wersen, Louis G. "The Challenge of Change." MUSIC EDUCATION JOURNAL 53:38-41, May, 1967.

Wilcoxson, I. "Faster Learning Through Singable Materials."
COLORADO JOURNAL OF RESEARCH IN MUSIC EDUCATION
1:26-27, Spring, 1964.

Wurtz, M. H. "Music for the Academically Talented High School
Student." MISSOURI JOURNAL OF RESEARCH IN MUSIC EDUCA-
TION 1,1:25-28, 1962.

Zaripov, R. K. "Cybernetics and Music." PERSPECTIVES OF NEW
MUSIC 7,2:115-154, Spring-Summer, 1969.

BOOKS

Bentley, Arnold. MUSICAL ABILITY IN CHILDREN AND ITS
MEASUREMENT. New York: October House, 1966.

Contemporary Music Project for Creativity in Music Education.
EXPERIMENTS IN MUSICAL CREATIVITY. Washington, D.C.:
Music Educator's National Conference, 1966.

Emerich, Paul. THE ROAD TO MODERN MUSIC. New York:
Southern Music Publishing Company, 1960.

Ferguson, Donald Nivison. THE WHY OF MUSIC; DIALOGUES IN
AN UNEXPLORED REGION OF APPRECIATION. Minneapolis:
University of Minnesota Press, 1969.

Garland, Phyl. THE SOUND OF SOUL. Regnery, November, 1969.

Hartshorn, W. C. MUSIC FOR THE ACADEMICALLY TALENTED
STUDENT. Washington, D.C.: MENC, 1960.

Hickman, Aubrey. ELECTRONIC APPARATUS FOR MUSIC RE-
SEARCH. London: Novello, 1968.

Hiller, Lejaren Arthur. EXPERIMENTAL MUSIC; COMPOSITION WITH AN ELECTRONIC COMPUTER. New York: McGraw-Hill, 1959.

Hutchings, A. THE INVENTION AND COMPOSITION OF MUSIC. London: Novello, 1958.

Marquis, G. Welton. TWENTIETH CENTURY MUSIC IDIOMS. Englewood Cliffs, New Jersey: Prentice Hall, 1964.

Paynter, John and Peter Ashton. SOUND AND SILENCE: CLASSROOM PROJECTS IN CREATIVE MUSIC. London: Cambridge University Press, 1970.

Russo, William. JAZZ COMPOSITION AND ORCHESTRATION. Chicago: University of Chicago Press, 1968.

Shuter, Rosamund. THE PSYCHOLOGY OF MUSICAL ABILITY. London: Methuen, 1968.

Thackray, R. M. CREATIVE MUSIC IN EDUCATION. London: Novello, 1966.

Walter, Samuel. MUSIC COMPOSITION AND ARRANGING. New York: Abingdon Press, 1965.

Werder, Richard Harry, ed. NEW CHALLENGES FOR MUSIC EDUCATION; PROCEEDINGS OF THE WORKSHOP...JUNE 11-22, 1964. Washington: Catholic University of America Press, 1965.

Wilkie, Richard W. QUEST FOR THE CREATIVE; AN ANALYTICAL REPORT OF A SEMINAR IN CREATIVE MUSIC AND THE RELATED ARTS FOR ELEMENTARY SCHOOL CHILDREN. Albany, Capital Area School Development Association. State University of New York at Albany, 1964.

CREATIVITY IN POETRY

PERIODICALS

"Authors and Editors; Found Poetry and Pop Poetry." PUBLISHERS'
WEEKLY 192:20-21, August 7, 1967.

Behn, Harry. "Definition Implied." HORN BOOK 43:561-564,
October, 1967.

Benedikt, Michael. "Completed Pattern." POETRY 109:262-267,
January, 1967.

Berry, Wendell. "Response to a War." NATION 204:527-528,
April 24, 1967.

Bly, Robert. "On Political Poetry." NATION 204:522-524,
April 24, 1967.

Braybrooke, Neville. "Poetry of Robert Lowell." CATHOLIC
WORLD 198:230-237, January, 1964.

Carruth, Hayden. "Ezra Pound and the Great Style." SATURDAY
REVIEW 49:21-22, 56, April 9, 1966.

---. "How Not to Rate a Poet." SATURDAY REVIEW 49:21, 43-44,
February 12, 1966.

Chapin, Katherine G. "Courage of Irony; Poetry of Allen Tate."
NEW REPUBLIC 153:22-24, July 24, 1965.

Ciardi, John. "Manner of Speaking: Definition of Poetry."

SATURDAY REVIEW 49:10, 12, September 17, 1966.

---. "Manner of Speaking; of Poetry and Sloganeering." SATURDAY REVIEW 51:14, January 6, 1968.

---. "Poetry and Personal Definition." SATURDAY REVIEW 48:41, October 9, 1965.

Clark, Thomas. "Zukofsky's ALL." POETRY 107:55-59, October, 1965.

Costa, Richard H. "Lowry-Aiken Symbiosis." NATION 204:823-826, June 26, 1967.

Cowley, Malcolm. "Pound Reweighed." REPORTER 24:35-36, 38-40, March 2, 1961.

Cutler, Bruce. "American Heart of Darkness." POETRY 107:401-403, March, 1966.

Davie, Donald. "After Sedley, after Pound." NATION 201:311-313, November 1, 1965.

Davison, Peter. "Difficulties of Being Major; the Poetry of Robert Lowell and James Dickey." ATLANTIC MONTHLY 220:116-121, October, 1967.

---. "Madness in the New Poetry." ATLANTIC MONTHLY 215:90-93, January, 1965.

---. "Self-revelation in the New Poetry." ATLANTIC MONTHLY 208:170-172, 174, November, 1961.

deToledano, Ralph. "Poetry of the Beats." NATIONAL REVIEW 11:346, 348-350, November 18, 1961.

Dickey, J. "Robert Frost, Man and Myth." ATLANTIC MONTHLY 218:53-56, November, 1966.

Di Cyan, Erwin. "Poetry and Creativeness: with Notes on the Role of Psychedelic Agents." PERSPECTIVES IN BIOLOGY AND MEDICINE 14:639-650, Summer, 1971.

Draper, R. P. "Form and Tone in the Poetry of D. H. Lawrence." ENGLISH STUDIES 49:498-508, December, 1968.

Elman, Richard M. "Poet of Plainness." COMMONWEAL 82:250-251, 254, May 14, 1965.

Fetler, Andrew. "Bloodless Man." ANTIOCH REVIEW 29:348-351, Fall, 1969.

Fiedler, Leslie A. "On the Road; of the Adventures of Karl Shapiro." POETRY 96:171-178, June, 1960.

Flint, R. W. "On Randall Jarrell ." COMMENTARY 47:79-81, February, 1966.

Frankel, Haskel. "One Brief, Shining Moment: Pop Poetry." SATURDAY REVIEW 50:22-23, September 2, 1967.

Fuller, John G. "Trade Winds." SATURDAY REVIEW 48:10-11, March 27, 1965.

Gerstel, Eva-Maria. "Creative Process in Two Early Manuscripts of Paul Valery's 'Fragments du Narcisse'." SYMPOSIUM 23:16-37, Spring, 1969.

Goldman, Michael. "Berryman; without Impudence and Vanity." NATION 208:245-246, February 24, 1969.

---. "Inventing the American Heart." NATION 204:529-530, April 24, 1967.

---. "Shoe in the Shark; National Poetry." NATION 202:246-248, February 28, 1966.

Graves, Robert. "Art of Poetry; Interview by Peter Buckman and

William Fifield." PARIS REVIEW pp. 118-145, Summer, 1969.

Hamilton, James W. "Object Loss, Dreaming, and Creativity: The Poetry of John Keats." PSYCHOANALYTIC STUDY OF THE CHILD 24:488-531, 1969.

Harrison, Jim. "California hybrid." POETRY 108:198-201, June, 1966.

---. "Northness of North." NATION 200:180, February 15, 1965.

Harrower, Molly. "Poems Emerging from the Therapeutic Experience." JOURNAL OF NERVOUS AND MENTAL DISEASE 149: 213-223, 1969.

Hartsook, John H. "Becquer and the Poetic Imagination." HISPANIC REVIEW 35:252-269, July, 1967.

Hicks, Granville. "Meeting the Geniune Mystery." SATURDAY REVIEW 48:15-16, July 31, 1965.

Howard, Richard. "Fuel on the Fire." POETRY 110:413-415, September, 1967.

---. "Illusion Wedded to Simple Need." POETRY 108:329-335, August, 1966.

---. "Two against Chaos." NATION 200:289-290, March 15, 1965.

Huxley, Aldous. "Only Way to Write a Modern Poem about a Nightingale." HARPER'S MAGAZINE 227:62-66, August, 1963.

Jacobsen, Josephine. "Legacy of Three Poets." COMMONWEAL 78:189-192, May 10, 1963.

---. "Poet of the Particular." COMMONWEAL 81:349-352, December 4, 1964.

Jaffe, Dan. "Voice of the Poet: Oracular, Eerie, Daring."

SATURDAY REVIEW 52:28-29, 62, September 6, 1969.

Kapp, F. T. "Ezra Pound's Creativity and Treason: Clues from His Life and Work." COMPREHENSIVE PSYCHIATRY 9:414-427, 1969.

Koch, Stephen. "Performance without a Net." NATION 204:524-526, April 24, 1967.

Kunitz, Stanley. "Roethke: Poet of Transformations." NEW REPUB-LIC 152:23-29, January 23, 1965.

Leavy, Stanley A. "John Keats's Psychology of Creative Imagination." PSYCHOANALYTIC QUARTERLY 39:173-197, 1970.

Lentricchia, Frank, Jr. "Some Coordinates of Modern Literature." POETRY 108:65-67, April, 1966.

---. "Wallace Stevens: the Ironic Eye." YALE REVIEW 56:336-353, Spring, 1967.

Lupton, Mary Jane. "The Dark Dream of 'Dejection'." LITERATURE AND PSYCHOLOGY 18:39-47, 1968.

MacShane, F. "New Poetry." AMERICAN SCHOLAR 37:642-646, Autumn, 1968.

Malanga, Gerard. "Some Thoughts on BOTTOM and AFTER I's." POETRY 107:60-64, October, 1965.

Michaelson, L. W. "View: On Anti-war Poetry." TRACE 68:222-224, 1968.

Moon, Samuel. "Master as Servant." POETRY 108:189-190, June, 1966.

Morse, D. E. "Avant-rock in the Classroom." ENGLISH JOURNAL 58:196-200, 297, February, 1969.

Murphy, Francis. "Going It Alone: Estrangement in American Poetry." YALE REVIEW 56:17-24, Autumn, 1966.

Pack, Robert. "To Be Loved for Its Voice." SATURDAY REVIEW 51:39-40, August 24, 1968.

Pearson, Norman Holmes. "Norman Holmes Pearson on H. D.: an Interview." CONTEMPORARY LITERATURE 10:435-446, Autumn, 1969.

"Poetry: Combatting Society with Surrealism." TIME 93:72, 74-E10, January 24, 1969.

Rago, Henry. "Vocation of Poetry"; address, November 28, 1966. POETRY 110:328-348, August, 1967.

Riddel, Joseph N. "H. D. and the Poetics of 'Spiritual Realism'." CONTEMPORARY LITERATURE 10:447-473, Autumn, 1969.

Robinson, J. "Celebration: the Lyric poetry of Melville Cane." AMERICAN SCHOLAR 38:286-296, Spring, 1969.

Rosenthal, M. L. "Couch and Poetic Insight." REPORTER 32:52-53, March 25, 1965.

Roth, Nathan. "Porphyria of Heinrich Heine." COMPREHENSIVE PSYCHIATRY 10:90-106, 1969.

Rukeyser, Muriel. "Crystal for the Metaphysical." SATURDAY REVIEW 49:52-53, 81, October 1, 1966.

Russell, Paul. "How to Sing of a Diminished Thing; Recent Works of Interesting Poets." SATURDAY REVIEW 48:30-32, July 3, 1965.

Scully, James. "Search for Passion." NATION 197:329-330, November 16, 1963.

"Second Chance." TIME 89:67-74, June 2, 1967.

Poetry

Simpson, Louis. "Dead Horses and Live Issues ?" NATION 204: 520-522, April 24, 1967.

Sorrentino, Gilbert. "World and Self: Instances." POETRY 106:306-309, July, 1965.

Spector, Robert D. "Way to Say What a Man Can See; Modern American and English Poetry." SATURDAY REVIEW 48:46-48, February 13, 1965.

Untermeyer, Louis. "Conrad Aiken: Our Best Known Unread Poet." SATURDAY REVIEW 50:28-29, 76-77, November 25, 1967.

---. "Way of Seeing and Saying." SATURDAY REVIEW 50:31, 55, May 6, 1967.

Wain, John . "New Robert Lowell." NEW REPUBLIC 151:21-23, October 17, 1964.

Walsh, Chad. "Cadence for Our Time." SATURDAY REVIEW 48: 28-30, January 2, 1965.

"War: Poetic Impressions." CHRISTIAN CENTURY 85:382-383, March 27, 1968.

Wesling, Donald. "Berkeley: Free Speech and Free Verse; Poetry Conference." NATION 201:338-340, November 8, 1965.

Whittemore, Reed. "The Two Rooms: Humor in Modern American Verse." WISCONSIN STUDIES IN CONTEMPORARY LITERATURE 5:185-191, Autumn, 1964.

Zweig, Paul. "Murderous Solvent." NATION 204:536-538, April 24, 1967.

---. "Music of Angels." NATION 208:311-313, March 10, 1969.

BOOKS

Adams, Hazard. THE CONTENTS OF POETRY. Boston: Little, Brown, 1963.

Bachelard, Gaston. THE POETICS OF SPACE. New York: Orion Press, 1964.

Bunn, James Harry. "Palace of Art: a Study of Form in Retrospective Poems about the Creative Process."Ph. D. dissertation. Emory University, 1969.

Cane, Melville. MAKING A POEM; AN INQUIRY INTO THE CREATIVE PROCESS. New York: Harcourt, Brace and World, 1963.

Carroll, Paul. THE POEM IN ITS SKIN. New York: Follett Publishing Company, 1968.

Charters, Samuel Barclay. THE POETRY OF THE BLUES. New York: Oak Publications, 1963.

Cowling, William Hammill. "Blake and the Redeemer Poet." Ph. D. dissertation. Indiana University, 1969.

Dembo, L. S. CONCEPTIONS OF REALITY IN MODERN AMERICAN POETRY. Berkeley and Los Angeles: University of California Press, 1966.

Dickey, James. BABEL TO BYZANTIUM; POETS AND POETRY NOW. New York: Farrar, Straus, and Giroux, 1968.

Donoghue, Denis. CONNOISSEURS OF CHAOS; IDEAS OF ORDER IN MODERN AMERICAN POETRY. New York: Macmillan, 1965.

Gambon, Glauco. THE INCLUSIVE FLAME; STUDIES IN AMERICAN POETRY. Bloomington: Indiana University Press, 1963.

Ghiselin, Brewster, ed. THE CREATIVE PROCESS; A SYMPOSIUM.
New York : New American Library, 1952 .

Gibson, Walker. POEMS IN THE MAKING. Boston: Houghton, 1963.

Gleckner, Robert F. "Blake's Verbal Technique." (In WILLIAM
BLAKE; ESSAYS FOR S. FOSTER DAMON, ed. by Alvin H.
Rosenfeld. Providence, Rhode Island: Brown University Press,
1969, pp. 321-332.)

Harding, Denys Clement Wyatt. EXPERIENCE INTO WORDS;
ESSAYS ON POETRY. New York: Horizon Press, 1964, pp.
175-197.

Holloway, John. THE LION HUNT; A PURSUIT OF POETRY AND
REALITY. Hamden, Connecticut: Archon Books, 1964.

Holmes, John. WRITING POETRY. Boston: Writer, Incorporated,
1960.

Howard, Richard. ALONE WITH AMERICA; ESSAYS ON THE ART
OF POETRY IN THE UNITED STATES SINCE 1950. New York:
Atheneum, 1969.

Hungerford, Edward Buell, ed. POETS IN PROGRESS; CRITICAL
PREFACES TO TEN CONTEMPORARY AMERICANS. Evanston,
Illinois : Northwestern University Press, 1962.

Jabbar, Abdul. "Keats' View of Poetry." Ph. D. dissertation.
Case Western Reserve University, 1969.

James, David Gwilym. SCEPTICISM AND POETRY; AN ESSAY ON
THE POETIC IMAGINATION. New York: Barnes and Noble, 1960.

Lewis, Clive Staples. "Psycho-analysis and Literary Criticism."
(In Lewis, C.S. SELECTED LITERARY ESSAYS. London: Cambridge, 1969, pp. 286-300.)

Linenthal, Mark, ed. ASPECTS OF POETRY; MODERN PERSPEC-

TIVES. Boston: Little, Brown, 1963.

Lowes, John Livingston. THE ROAD TO ZANADU; A STUDY IN THE WAYS OF THE IMAGINATION. Boston and New York: Houghton Mifflin, 1927.

Lutyens, David B. THE CREATIVE ENCOUNTER. London: Secker and Warburg, 1960.

MacLeish, Archibald. POETRY AND EXPERIENCE. Cambridge: Riverside Press, 1961.

McLuhan , Herbert Marshall. "Wyndham Lewis; His Theory of Art and Communication." (In McLuhan, H.M. THE INTERIOR LANDSCAPE; THE LITERARY CRITICISM OF MARSHALL MCLUHAN 1943-1962. New York: McGraw Hill, 1969, pp. 83-94.)

Major, Clarence, comp. THE NEW BLACK POETRY. New York: International Publishers, 1969.

Mazzaro, Jerome, comp. MODERN AMERICAN POETRY; ESSAYS IN CRITICISM. New York: David McKay,   1970 .

Miller, Joseph J. POETS OF REALITY; SIX TWENTIETH-CENTURY WRITERS. Cambridge: Belknap Press, 1965.

Mills, Ralph J. CONTEMPORARY AMERICAN POETRY. New York: Random House, 1965.

Moraze, Charles. "Literary Invention." (In Macksey, Richard and Donoto, Eugenio Umberto, eds. THE LANGUAGE OF CRITICISM AND THE SCIENCES OF MAN; THE STRUCTURALIST CON-TROVERSY. Baltimore: Johns Hopkins Press, 1970, pp. 22-33.)

Nemerov, Howard, ed. POETS ON POETRY. New York: Basic Books, 1966.

O'Brien, Mary Patricia. "Theme of Human Communication in the Poetry of Carlos Drummond de Andrade." Ph. D. dissertation, a

Poetry

portion of the text in Portuguese. Tulane University, 1969.

Ossman, David. THE SULLEN ART; INTERVIEWS WITH MODERN
AMERICAN POETS. New York: Corinth Books, 1963.

Read, Sir Herbert Edward. "Vico and the Genetic Theory of Poetry."
In Tagliacozzo, Giorgio and White, Haydon V., eds. GIAMBAT-
TISTA VICO. Baltimore: Hopkins Press, 1969, pp. 591-597.

Rees, Garnet. "Baudelaire and the Imagination." (In MODERN
MISCELLANY PRESENTED TO EUGENE VINAVER. New York:
Barnes and Noble, 1969, pp. 203-215.)

Rivers, Isabel. "Poetry of Conservation, 1600-1745; Jonson,
Dryden, and Pope." Ph.D. dissertation. Columbia University,
1969.

Rosenheim, Edward W. WHAT HAPPENED IN LITERATURE; A
STUDENT'S GUIDE TO POETRY, DRAMA AND FICTION.
Chicago: University of Chicago Press, 1960.

Ruihley, Glenn Richard. "Amy Lowell; Symbolic Impressionist."
Ph. D. dissertation. University of Wisconsin, 1969.

Schwartz, Delmore. "Views of a Second Violinist; Some Answers
to Questions about Writing Poetry." (In Schwartz, Delmore.
SELECTED ESSAYS OF DELMORE SCHWARTZ. Chicago:
University of Chicago Press, 1970, pp.224-229.)

Sewell, Elizabeth. "Bacon, Vico, Coleridge, and the Poetic
Method." (In Tagliacozzo, Giorgio and White, Haydon V., eds.
GIAMBATTISTA VICO. Baltimore: Johns Hopkins Press, 1969,
pp. 125-136.)

---. THE HUMAN METAPHOR. Notre Dame, Indiana: University of
Notre Dame, 1964.

Stepanchev, Stephen. AMERICAN POETRY SINCE 1945: A CRITICAL
SURVEY. New York: Harper and Row, 1965.

Sullivan, Nancy. PERSPECTIVE AND THE POETIC PROCESS. The Hague, Paris: Mouton, 1968.

Sweeney, Richard Monnett. " 'Editur Ez' and 'Old Hugger-Scrunch': the Influence of Ezra Pound on the Poems of William Carlos Williams." Ph. D. dissertation. Brown University, 1969.

Unger, Leonard, ed. SEVEN MODERN AMERICAN POETS; AN INTRODUCTION. Minneapolis: University of Minnesota Press, 1967.

CREATIVITY IN SPEECH COMMUNICATION

PERIODICALS

Abraham, Henry J. "Freedom of Expression: A Constant Dilemma."
SOCIAL EDUCATION 23:364-370, 382, December, 1959.

Auer, J. Jeffery. "Speech Is a Social Force." NEA JOURNAL
49:21-23, November, 1960.

Baker, Virgil L. "Role of Human Values in Communication."
VITAL SPEECHES 31:434-437, May 1, 1965.

Bunn, Charles. "How Lawyers Use Speech." SPEECH TEACHER
13:6-9, January, 1964.

Fadiman, William. "Lingua California Spoken Here." SATURDAY
REVIEW 45:19-20, November 17, 1962.

Ganguly, S. N. "Culture, Communication, and Silence." PHILOS-
OPHY AND PHENOMONOLOGICAL RESEARCH 29:182-200,
December, 1968.

Gibson, James W. "Creativity in the Speech Classroom." CENTRAL
STATES SPEECH JOURNAL 15:129-133, May, 1964.

Golden, Ruth I. "Speaking the Same Language; Folk Speech of
Negroes and Disadvantaged White Migrants." NEA JOURNAL
56:40, 53-54, 56, 58, March, 1967.

Green, William D. "Language and the Culturally Different."
ENGLISH JOURNAL 54:724-733, November, 1965.

Gruner, Charles R. "An Experimental Study of Satire as Persuasion." SPEECH MONOGRAPHS 32:149-153, June, 1965.

Haiman, Franklyn S. "Rhetoric of the Streets: Some Legal and Ethical Considerations." QUARTERLY JOURNAL OF SPEECH 53:99-114, April, 1967.

Hockett, Charles F. "Origin of Speech." SCIENTIFIC AMERICAN 203:88-96, September, 1960.

Langer, Susanne K. "Origins of Speech and Its Communicative Function." QUARTERLY JOURNAL OF SPEECH 46:121-134, April, 1960.

"Language Understanding Could Be Hereditary." SCIENCE NEWS LETTER 82:352, December 1, 1962.

McCroskey, James C. "The Effects of Evidence in Persuasive Communication." WESTERN SPEECH 31:189-199, Summer, 1967.

Maier, Norman R. F , Mara Julius, and James A. Thurber. "Studies in Creativity: Individual Differences in the Storing and Utilization of Information." AMERICAN JOURNAL OF PSYCHOLOGY 80:492-519, December, 1967.

Monaghan, Robert R. "A Systematic Way of Being Creative." JOURNAL OF COMMUNICATION 18:47-56, March, 1968.

O'Brien, Harold J. "How to Think Creatively." TODAY'S SPEECH 5:17-19, November, 1957.

Pei, Mario. "English in 2061: A Forecast." SATURDAY REVIEW 44:12-14, January 14, 1961.

---. "Hidden Politics of Words; Colonialism of Language." SATURDAY REVIEW 49:22-24, January 15, 1966.

Petras, James. "Politics of Democracy: The Free Speech Movement; a Student Comments on the Significance of the Berkeley Revolution;

with a Faculty Defense of the Student Position." PHI DELTA KAPPAN 46:343-346, March, 1965.

Searle, John R. "Meaning and Speech Acts." PHILOSOPHICAL REVIEW 71:423-432, October, 1962.

Smith, Ewart E. and Helen L. White. "Wit, Creativity, and Sarcasm." JOURNAL OF APPLIED PSYCHOLOGY 49:131-134, April, 1965.

Strawson, P. F. "Intention and Convention in Speech Acts." PHILOSOPHICAL REVIEW 73:439-460, October, 1964.

Tedford, Thomas L. "Teaching Freedom of Speech Through the Use of Common Materials." SPEECH TEACHER 16:269-270, November, 1967.

Weaver, Andrew Thomas. "Toward Understanding Through Speech." VITAL SPEECHES 27:244-247, February 1, 1961.

Wieman, Henry N. "The Philosophical Significance of Speech." CENTRAL STATES SPEECH JOURNAL 12:170-175, Spring, 1961.

Will, Frederick L. "Language, Usage, and Judgment." ANTIOCH REVIEW 23:273-290, Fall, 1963.

BOOKS

Bormann, Ernest G. THEORY AND RESEARCH IN THE COMMUNICATIVE ARTS. New York: Holt, Rinehart and Winston, 1965.

Brandes, Paul Dickerson and William S. Smith. BUILDING BETTER SPEECH. New York: Noble and Noble, 1962.

Brown, Charles T. and Charles Van Riper. SPEECH AND MAN.

Englewood Cliffs, New Jersey: Prentice-Hall, 1966.

Capp, Glenn Richard. HOW TO COMMUNICATE ORALLY. 2nd ed. Englewood Cliffs, New Jersey: Prentice-Hall, 1966.

Chouchard, Paul. LANGUAGE AND THOUGHT. New York: Walker, 1964.

Dance, Frank E. X., ed. HUMAN COMMUNICATION THEORY: ORIGINAL ESSAYS. New York: Holt, Rinehart and Winston, 1967.

Dickens, Milton. SPEECH: DYNAMIC COMMUNICATION. New York: Harcourt, Brace, 1954.

Eisenson, Jon, J. Jeffery Auer, and John V. Irwin. THE PSYCHOLOGY OF COMMUNICATION. New York: Appleton-Century-Crofts, 1963.

Eisler, Frieda Goldman. PSYCHOLINGUISTICS: EXPERIMENTS IN SPONTANEOUS SPEECH. New York: Academic Press, 1968.

Fest, Thorrel B. and Martin T. Cobin. SPEECH AND THEATER. Washington: Center for Applied Research in Education, 1964.

Garrison, Webb B. CREATIVE IMAGINATION IN PREACHING. New York: Abingdon Press, 1960.

Geldard, Frank A., ed. COMMUNICATION PROCESSES. New York: Macmillan, 1966.

Hedde, Wilhelmina G., William Norwood Brigance, and Victor M. Powell. THE NEW AMERICAN SPEECH. 3rd ed. Philadelphia: Lippincott, 1968.

Hunsinger, Paul. COMMUNICATIVE INTERPRETATION. Dubuque, Iowa: W. C. Brown Company, 1967.

Hylton, Carroll G. "The Effects of Observable Audience Response on Attitude Change and Source Credibility." Ph. D. dissertation. Michigan State University, 1968.

Kwant, Remigius C. PHENOMENOLOGY OF LANGUAGE.

Pittsburgh: Duquesne University Press, 1965.

LaRusso, Dominic A. BASIC SKILLS OF ORAL COMMUNICATION. Dubuque, Iowa: W. C. Brown Company, 1967.

Machlin, Evangeline. SPEECH FOR THE STAGE. New York: Theatre Arts Books, 1966.

McLuhan, Herbert Marshall. UNDERSTANDING MEDIA: THE EXTENSIONS OF MAN. New York: McGraw-Hill, 1964.

Meerloo, Joost Abraham Maurits. CONVERSATION AND COMMUNICATION: A PSYCHOLOGICAL INQUIRY INTO LANGUAGE AND HUMAN RELATIONS. New York: International Universities Press, 1952.

Miller, George A. THE PSYCHOLOGY OF COMMUNICATION: SEVEN ESSAYS. New York: Basic Books, 1967.

Oliver, Robert Tarbell, Harold P. Zelko, and Paul D. Holtzman. COMMUNICATIVE SPEAKING AND LISTENING. 4th ed. New York: Holt, Rinehart and Winston, 1968.

Phillips, David and Jack Hall Lamb. SPEECH AS COMMUNICATION. Boston: Allyn and Bacon, 1966.

Rich, Andrea L. "An Experimental Study of the Nature of Communication to a Deviate in High and Low Cohesive Groups." Ph. D. dissertation, University of California, Los Angeles, 1968.

Ross, Raymond Samuel. SPEECH COMMUNICATION; FUNDAMENTALS AND PRACTICE. 2nd ed. Englewood Cliffs, New Jersey: Prentice-Hall, 1970.

St. Onge, Keith R. CREATIVE SPEECH. Belmont, California: Wadsworth Publishing Company, 1964.

Salcedo, Rodolfo N. "A Communication Model of Modernization." Ph. D. dissertation. Michigan State University, 1968.

Samovar, Larry A. and Jack Mills. ORAL COMMUNICATION: MESSAGE AND RESPONSE. Dubuque, Iowa: W. C. Brown Company, 1968.

Sandford, William Phillips and Willard Hayes Yeager. PRINCIPLES OF EFFECTIVE SPEAKING. 6th ed. New York: Ronald Press Company, 1963.

Smith, Alfred G., ed. COMMUNICATION AND CULTURE. New York: Holt, Rinehart and Winston, 1966.

Tepper, Albert and Paul A. Roman. THE ORAL COMMUNICATOR; HIS ROLE AND FUNCTION. Minneapolis: Burgess Publishing Company, 1968.

Venderbush, Kenneth Ray. "Communication in Contemporary Student Controversies." Ph. D. dissertation, Ohio State University, 1968.

Walter, Otis M. and Robert L. Scott. THINKING AND SPEAKING; A GUIDE TO INTELLIGENT ORAL COMMUNICATION. 2nd ed. New York: Macmillan, 1968.

CREATIVITY IN THEATRE

PERIODICALS

Abel, Lionel. "Theatre of Politics: The Negro." NATION 196:
351-354, April 27, 1963.

Atcheson, Richard. "My God, They're Naked!" HOLIDAY 44:46-
49, 118, November, 1968.

---. "Theater of Involvement." HOLIDAY 44:60-61, 82, 84-85,
October, 1968.

Atkins, Thomas R. "Theater of Possibilities." KENYON REVIEW
30,2:274-281, 1968.

Bailey, Peter. "Black Theater." EBONY 24:126-128, 130-132, 134,
August, 1969.

---. "Importance of Being Black." NEWSWEEK 73:102-103,
February 24, 1969.

Barnes, Clive. "Successful Musical Combines the Sound of Today
with a Nonexistent Story." HOLIDAY 45:12, 17-18, March, 1969.

Benedetti, Robert. "Metanaturalism: The Metaphorical Use of
Environment in the Modern Theatre." CHICAGO REVIEW 17,2-3:
24-32, 1964.

Bentley, Eric. "Naked Reality." NEW REPUBLIC 161:31-34,
August 9, 1969.

---. "Problem of Modern Drama." NEW REPUBLIC 135:22-23, August 13, 1956.

---. "Theatre of Interpretations; the Documentary Play." NATION 209:148-149, 151, August 25, 1969.

Boyd, John. "Christian Imagination in Two Modern Dramas." AMERICA 119:621-624, December 14, 1968.

Brecht, Stefan. "Family of the f. p.--Notes on the Theatre of the Ridiculous." DRAMA REVIEW 13:117-141, Fall, 1968.

Brustein, Robert. "Third Theater That Is Superb, Gay and Wild." NEW YORK TIMES MAGAZINE pp. 32-33, 92, 94, 96, 99-100, 102, 104, September 25, 1966.

---. "Two Revolutions: Negro and Sexual (or Homosexual)." NEW REPUBLIC 152:26-27, March 27, 1965.

---. "We Are Two Cultural Nations." NEW REPUBLIC 151:25-26, 28, 30, November 21, 1964.

"Burst of Negro Drama." LIFE 56:62-70, May 29, 1964.

Clurman, Harold. "Frightened Fifties and Onward." THEATRE ARTS 45:12-13, 77, March, 1961.

Clurman, Harold and Digby Diehl. "The Idea of the Theatre." TRANSATLANTIC REVIEW 16:17-24, Summer, 1964.

Cobin, Martin T. "Criticism in Teaching; Oral Interpretation and Drama." WESTERN SPEECH JOURNAL 28:27-34, Winter, 1964.

Colimore, Benjamin. " 'Paradise Now'?: An Essay on the Living Theater." CATHOLIC WORLD 209:30-34, April, 1969.

"Comedy: A Sharp-Cornered Round-Table Discussion by Five Celebrated Authors of Stage Comedy." VOGUE 152:228-229, 257-260, 264, October 1, 1968.

Theatre

Driver, Tom F. "Search for Conflict." NATION 194:350-354,
April 21, 1962.

Esslin, Martin. "New Form in the Theatre." NATION 192:342-344,
April 22, 1961.

Fleissner, E. M. "Revolution as Theatre: DANTON'S DEATH and
MARAT/SADE." MASSACHUSETTS REVIEW 7,3:543-556, Summer,
1966.

Gianakaris, C. J. "Absurdism Altered: ROSENCRANTZ AND
GUILDENSTERN ARE DEAD." DRAMA SURVEY 7:52-58,
Winter, 1968-1969.

Gilman, Richard. "Theater of Ignorance; Living Theater." ATLAN-
TIC MONTHLY 224:35-42, July, 1969.

Goldstein, Malcolm. "Body and Soul on Broadway." MODERN
DRAMA 7:411-421, February, 1965.

Hadden, Jane. "Developing Creativity Through Dramatization."
CENTRAL STATES SPEECH JOURNAL 7:28-32, Spring, 1956.

Halprin, Ann. "Ceremony of US." DRAMA REVIEW 13:131-143,
Summer, 1969.

---. "Mutual Creation." DRAMA REVIEW 13:163-172, Fall, 1968.

Hatch, Robert. "Case for Repertory." HORIZON 5:106-109,
January, 1963.

---. "Hunt for Heroes." HORIZON 4:110-112, May, 1962.

---. "Laugh Now, Pay Later." HORIZON 5:106-109, March, 1963.

---. "Where There is Total Involvement; the Living Theatre."
HORIZON 4:106-109, March, 1962.

Hewes, Henry. "Government by the Unelected." SATURDAY

REVIEW 52:16, September 13, 1969.

Hirsch, S. "Theatre of the Absurd (Made in America)." JOURNAL
OF SOCIAL ISSUES 20:49-61, January, 1964.

Hivnor, Mary O. "Adaptations and Adaptors." KENYON REVIEW
30,2:265-273, 1968.

Hughes, Catharine R. "Theatre of Ritual?" AMERICA 121:160-161,
September 13, 1969.

---. "Where Are The Playwrights?" NATION 208:90-93, January
20, 1969.

Junker, Howard. "Group Theater; Open Theatre." NEWSWEEK 73:
128, 133, May 26, 1969.

Kaplan, Donald M. "Homosexuality and American Theatre: A
Psychoanalytic Comment." TULANE DRAMA REVIEW 9:25-55,
Spring, 1965.

Kase, J. B. "Theatre Resources for Youth in New Hampshire:
PACE Project." EDUCATIONAL THEATRE JOURNAL 21:205-
213, May, 1969.

Kerr, Jean. "What Happens Out of Town; Trying Out a Show."
HARPER'S MAGAZINE 220:37-40, June, 1960.

Kerr, Walter. "Making a Cult of Confusion; Theatre of the Absurd."
HORIZON 5:33-41, September, 1962.

---. "Participatory Theater." HARPER'S MAGAZINE 239:24, 26,
28, 30, 32, 34, 36, 38, 40, 43, October, 1969.

---. "What Can They Do for an Encore? Theater of Nudity."
NEW YORK TIMES MAGAZINE pp. 24-25, 26B, 28, 30, February
2, 1969.

King, Woodie, Jr. "Black Theatre: Present Condition." DRAMA

Theatre

REVIEW 12:117-124, Summer, 1968.

Kirby, Michael. "New Theatre." TULANE DRAMA REVIEW 10:23-43, Winter, 1965.

---. "Uses of Film in the New Theatre." TULANE DRAMA REVIEW 11:49-61, Fall, 1966.

Klingsick, J. "Ideas in Motion-Youth Theater: a Growing Expression of Creativity." YOUNG CHILDREN 23:324-328, September, 1968.

Kronenberger, Louis. "Time for Comedy." ATLANTIC MONTHLY 219:63-66, May, 1967.

Lamb, Howard. "Role Playing." TODAY'S EDUCATION 58:67-68, January, 1969.

Lamont, Rosette. "Death and Tragi-Comedy: Three Plays of the New Theatre." MASSACHUSETTS REVIEW 6,2:381-402, Winter-Spring, 1965.

Leary, Daniel J. "Theater of Dislike; Contemporary Drama." CATHOLIC WORLD 205:217-222, July, 1967.

Lester, Elenore. "Final Decline and Total Collapse of the American Avant-garde." ESQUIRE 71:142-143, 148-149, 176, 178, May, 1969.

Lewis, Theophilus. "Repertory Headaches." AMERICA 117:284-285, September 16, 1967.

Leyburn, Ellen Douglass. "Comedy and Tragedy Transposed: Modern Drama." YALE REVIEW 53:553-562, June, 1964.

MacOwan, Michael. "Why the Theatre?" DRAMA 93:38-42, Summer, 1969.

McWhirter, William A. "Revolution by Brother Alexis." LIFE

66:67-68, 69-70, January 31, 1969.

Mannes, Marya. "Half-World of American Drama." REPORTER 28: 48-50, April 25, 1963.

Martin, Paulette. "Theater of Mystery; from the Absurd to the Religious." COMMONWEAL 84:582-585, September 16, 1966.

Miller, Arthur. "State of the Theatre." HARPER'S MAGAZINE 221:63-69, November, 1960.

"Modern Theater or, The World as a Metaphor of Dread." TIME 88:34-35, July 8, 1966.

Mussoff, Lenore. "The Medium Is the Absurd." ENGLISH JOURNAL 58:566-570, 576, April, 1969.

Novick, Julius. "Pacific Coast; Postwar Resident Professional Theatres." NATION 202:755-758, June 20, 1966.

"On the Ball." NEWSWEEK 70:118, 121, November 20, 1967.

"Paperback of Broadway; Summer Stock Theater." NEWSWEEK 74: 78-79, August 4, 1969.

Prideaux, Tom. "They All Keep on Looking for Floogle Street." LIFE 51:79-83, July 28, 1961.

Richardson, Jack. "Groping Toward Freedom: The Living Theatre." COMMENTARY 47:79-81, May, 1969.

"Rise of Rep." TIME 83:54-61, February 14, 1964.

Rollman-Branch, Hilda S. "Psychical Reality and the Theater of Fact; Documentary Drama." AMERICAN IMAGO 26:56-70, Spring, 1969.

Schechner, Richard. "Containment Is the Enemy." DRAMA REVIEW 13:24-44, Spring, 1969.

Theatre

---. "Six Axioms for Environmental Theatre." DRAMA REVIEW 12:41-64, Spring, 1968.

---. "Speculations on Radicalism, Sexuality, and Performance." DRAMA REVIEW 13:89-110, Summer, 1969.

Schneck, Stephen. "Le Living." RAMPARTS MAGAZINE 7:34-41, November 30, 1968.

Schwartz, Alan U. "What Price Salvation? Theatre and the Law." THEATRE ARTS 46:65-66, September, 1962.

Seda Bonilla, Eduardo. "Spiritualism, Psychoanalysis, and Psychodrama." AMERICAN ANTHROPOLOGIST 71:493-497, June, 1969.

Sheehan, Peter J. "Theater of the Absurd: A Child Studies Himself." ENGLISH JOURNAL 58:561-565, April, 1969.

Silber, Irwin. "To: Julian Beck, Judith Malina, and the Living Theatre." DRAMA REVIEW 13:86-89, Spring, 1969.

Simon, John. "Tragedy of American Theater." HOLIDAY 39:76-83, 169, 171, 173-174, 176-177, March, 1966.

Stillman, Leonard. "Who Said the Revue Is Bad?" THEATRE ARTS 45:17-19, 76, March, 1961.

Sutherland, Elizabeth. "Theatre of the Meaningful." NATION 199: 254-256, October 19, 1964.

Thurber, James. "Future, If Any, of Comedy; or, Where Do We Non-Go from Here?" HARPER'S MAGAZINE 223:40-45, December, 1961.

Todd, Arthur. "What Makes a Musical Move?" THEATRE ARTS 44:66-67, 72, November, 1960.

Trotta, Gerk. "Black Theatre." HARPER'S BAZAAR 101:150-153, August, 1968.

The Communicative Arts

Weales, Gerald. "Off-Broadway: Its Contribution to American
Drama." DRAMA SURVEY 2:5-23, June, 1962.

Wellworth, George E. "Hope Deferred: The New American Drama.
Reflections on Edward Albee, Jack Richardson, Jack Gelber,
and Arthur Kopit." LITERARY REVIEW 7:7-26, Autumn, 1963.

Wildman, Eugene. "Reality Theater in Chicago." CHICAGO REVIEW
20:81-92, June, 1968.

Wodehouse, P. G. "What's Wrong?" THEATRE ARTS 44:8-9,
June, 1960.

Young, Stark. "Art of Theatre Criticism." HARPER'S MAGAZINE
220:26, 28-31, March, 1960.

BOOKS

Abel, Lionel. METATHEATRE. New York: Hill and Wang, 1963.

Albright, H. D., W. P. Halstead, and Lee Mitchell. PRINCIPLES
OF THEATRE ARTS. 2nd ed. Boston: Houghton Mifflin Company,
1968.

Bentley, Eric Russell. THE LIFE OF THE DRAMA. New York:
Atheneum, 1964.

---. THE THEATRE OF COMMITMENT, AND OTHER ESSAYS ON
DRAMA IN OUR SOCIETY. New York: Atheneum, 1967.

Bigsby, C. W. E. CONFRONTATION AND COMMITMENT: A STUDY
OF AMERICAN DRAMA, 1959-66. Columbia: University of
Missouri Press, 1968.

Blau, Herbert. THE IMPOSSIBLE THEATER, A MANIFESTO. New York: Macmillan, 1964.

Brook, Peter. THE EMPTY SPACE. New York: Atheneum, 1968.

Brustein, Robert. THE THEATRE OF REVOLT. Boston: Little, Brown and Company, 1964.

---. THE THIRD THEATRE. New York: Knopf, 1969.

Cameron, Kenneth M. and Theodore J. C. Hoffman. THE THEATRICAL RESPONSE. New York: Macmillan, 1969.

Clay, James H. and Daniel Krempel. THE THEATRICAL IMAGE. New York: McGraw-Hill, 1967.

Clurman, Harold. THE NAKED IMAGE: OBSERVATIONS ON THE MODERN THEATRE. New York: Macmillan, 1966.

Corrigan, Robert W. COMEDY MEANING AND FORM. San Francisco: Chandler Publishing Company, 1965.

---, ed. THE CONTEXT AND CRAFT OF DRAMA; CRITICAL ESSAYS ON THE NATURE OF DRAMA AND THEATRE. San Francisco: Chandler Publishing Company, 1964.

---. TRAGEDY VISION AND FORM. San Francisco: Chandler Publishing Company, 1965.

Culp, Ralph Borden. THE THEATRE AND ITS DRAMA. Dubuque, Iowa: William C. Brown Company, 1971.

Downer, Alan S. THE AMERICAN THEATER TODAY. New York: Basic Books, 1967.

Esslin, Martin. REFLECTIONS: ESSAYS ON MODERN THEATRE. Garden City, New York: Doubleday, 1969.

Gard, Robert E. THEATRE IN AMERICA. Madison, Wisconsin:

Dembar Educational Research Services, 1968.

Gassner, John. DIRECTIONS IN MODERN THEATRE AND DRAMA. New York: Holt, Rinehart and Winston, 1966.

Goldman, William. THE SEASON: A CANDID LOOK AT BROADWAY. New York: Harcourt, Brace and World, 1969.

Guthrie, Sir Tyrone. IN VARIOUS DIRECTIONS: A VIEW OF THEATRE. New York: Macmillan, 1965.

Kaufmann, Walter. TRAGEDY AND PHILOSOPHY. Garden City, New York: Doubleday, 1968.

Kernan, Alvin B., comp. THE MODERN AMERICAN THEATER: A COLLECTION OF CRITICAL ESSAYS. Englewood Cliffs, New Jersey: Prentice-Hall, 1967.

Kernodle, George and Portia. INVITATION TO THE THEATRE. New York: Harcourt Brace Jovanovitch, 1971.

Kerr, Walter, THE THEATRE IN SPITE OF ITSELF. New York: Simon and Schuster, 1963.

---. THIRTY PLAYS HATH NOVEMBER: PAIN AND PLEASURE IN THE CONTEMPORARY THEATRE. New York: Simon and Schuster, 1969.

Kirby, E. T., ed. TOTAL THEATRE: A CRITICAL ANTHOLOGY. New York: Dutton, 1969.

Kostelanetz, Richard. THE THEATRE OF MIXED MEANS: AN INTRODUCTION TO HAPPENINGS, KINETIC ENVIRONMENTS, AND OTHER MIXED-MEANS PERFORMANCES. New York: Dial Press, 1968.

Lewis, Allen. AMERICAN PLAYS AND PLAYWRIGHTS OF THE CONTEMPORARY THEATRE. New York: Crown Publishers, 1966.

Theatre

Mitchell, Loften. BLACK DRAMA: THE STORY OF THE AMERICAN NEGRO IN THE THEATRE. New York: Hawthorn Books, 1967.

Nicoll, Allardyce. THE THEATRE AND DRAMATIC THEORY. New York: Barnes and Noble, 1962.

Nicovich, George P. "Satire in Modern American Drama: 1918 to the Present." Ph. D. dissertation. University of Colorado, 1968.

Olson, Elder. TRAGEDY AND THE THEORY OF DRAMA. Detroit: Wayne State University Press, 1961.

Price, Julia S. THE OFF-BROADWAY THEATRE. New York: Scarecrow Press, 1962.

Rice, Elmer L. THE LIVING THEATRE. New York: Harper, 1959.

Schechner, Richard. PUBLIC DOMAIN: ESSAYS ON THE THEATER. Indianapolis: Bobbs-Merrill, 1969.

Schroeder, Robert J., ed. THE NEW UNDERGROUND THEATRE. New York: Bantam, 1968.

Selden, Samuel. THEATRE DOUBLE GAME. Chapel Hill: University of North Carolina Press, 1969.

Shank, Theodore Junior. THE ART OF DRAMATIC ART. Belmont, California: Dickenson Publishing Company, 1969.

Taylor, William E. MODERN AMERICAN DRAMA: ESSAYS IN CRITICISM. Deland, Florida: Everett/Edwards, 1968.

Valency, Maurice. THE FLOWER AND THE CASTLE. New York: Grosset and Dunlap, 1966.

Weales, Gerald. AMERICAN DRAMA SINCE WORLD WAR II. New York: Harcourt, Brace and World, 1962.

---. THE JUMPING-OFF PLACE: AMERICAN DRAMA IN THE

1960's. New York: Macmillan, 1969.

Weissman, Philip. CREATIVITY IN THE THEATRE; A PSYCHO-ANALYTIC STUDY. New York: Basic Books, 1965.

INDEX OF AUTHORS

Beardsley, Monroe C., 10
Beasley, N., 57
Beauchamp, James, 82
Beck, L. F., 65
Behn, Harry, 91
Beittel, K. R., 11
Beja, Morris, 39
Beloff, John, 10
Benedetti, Robert, 109
Benedikt, Michael, 91
Bentley, Arnold, 89
Bentley, Eric, 109, 116
Berdiaev, Nikolai Aleksandrovich, 27
Bergan, John R., 77
Berger, Donald P., 77
Berger, Ivan, 78
Berkovitz, Robert, 78
Berlin, Irving N., 10
Bernheimer, Martin, 78
Berry, S. N., 1
Berry, Wendell, 91
Bezanker, Abraham, 39
Bickford, John H., 10
Bigsby, C. W. E., 116
Birnbaum, M., 55
Birney, Earle, 46
Bishop, Jerry E., 65
Blackburn, T. E., 65
Bland, T. A., 65
Blank, D. M., 66
Blank, L., 55
Blau, Herbert, 117
Blumberg, A., 62
Blundell, William E., 66
Bly, Robert, 91
Bormann, Ernest G., 105
Bone, Robert A., 46
Boodish, H. M., 66
Booth, Wayne, 46
Boyd, John, 110

Boyers, Roberts, 39
Boretz, Benjamin, 78
Bowers, Faubion, 78
Boyle, R. P., 31
Brace, Gerald Warner, 47
Bradley, Duane, 75
Brandes, Paul Dickerson, 105
Brashers, Howard Charles, 47
Braybrooke, Neville, 91
Brecht, Stefan, 110
Bressler, H., 1
Brien, Alan, 11
Brigance, William Norwood, 106
Brittain, W. Lambert, 11, 27, 28
Brodzky, Anne, 11
Brook, Peter, 117
Brossard, Chandler, 39
Brown, Charles T., 105
Brown, Elwood Hansel, 78
Brown, R. L., 55
Brown, Stanley, 66
Brustein, Robert, 110, 117
Bryson, Lyman, 11
Buchman, S. J., 55
Bunn, Charles, 103
Bunn, James Harry, 98
Bunzel, P., 51
Burgess, Anthony, 39
Burgstahler, E. E., 78
Burton, John, 11
Buszak, B., 2
Butler, Reginald Cotterall, 27
Butor, Michel, 11
Byerly, Kenneth R., 66

Cain, M. E., 55
Calas, Nicholas, 11
Calkins, E. E., 2
Calsbeek, F., 55

123

Friedman, L., 3
Frisch, Bruce H., 81
Fry, Roger Eliot, 13
Fuller, John G., 93
Fuller, Richard Buckminster,
   13, 81

Gallagher, J. J., 33
Galloway, David D., 41
Gambon, Glauco, 98
Ganguly, S. N., 103
Gard, Robert E., 117
Garber, G. E., 33
Garis, Robert, 41, 52
Garland, Phyl, 89
Garnder, Martin, 67
Garrison, Webb B., 106
Garvin, W. Lawrence, 14
Gassner, John, 118
Gavagan, Peter C., 14
Geier, J. G., 57
Geismar, Maxwell, 41
Geldard, Frank, 106
Gerard, H. B., 62
Gerhardt, Mia I., 41
Gerstel, Eva-Maria, 93
Gerstel, Judith, 81
Getchell, J. S., 3
Getzels, Jacob W., 14, 28
Ghiselin, Brewster, 99
Gianakaris, C. J., 111
Gibson, James W., 67, 103
Gibson, Walker, 99
Giles, Allen, 81
Gill, B., 52
Gill, J. E., 33
Gillion, M. E., 67
Gilman, Richard, 14, 111
Glanville-Hicks, Peggy, 81
Glatzer, Robert, 7

Gleckner, Robert F., 99
Gold, Herbert, 41
Goldberg, A. A., 61
Golden, Ruth I., 103
Goldin, Amy, 14
Goldman, Michael, 93
Goldman, William, 118
Goldstein, I., 33
Goldstein, Malcolm, 111
Golembiewski, R. T., 62
Gombrich, Ernst Hans Josef, 14
Goodman, P., 33
Gordon, Jan B., 14
Gordon, M. W., 52
Gossage, H. L., 3
Goulet, R. R., 33
Graves, Robert, 93
Gray, C. E., 57
Green, William D., 103
Greenberg, Alvin, 41
Grispino, 33
Groch, Judith, 28
Gross, L. S., 33
Gross, Robert A., 41
Grossman, Manuel L., 14
Grubb, C. Norton, 68
Grumbach, Doris, 41
Gruner, Charles R., 104
Guenter, R. F., 12
Guthrie, Sir Tyrone, 118

Hadden, Jane, 111
Haiman, Franklyn S., 104
Hale, Nancy, 42
Hall, W. B., 3
Hallman, Ralph J., 14
Halprin, Ann, 111
Halprin, Lawrence, 47
Halstead, W. P., 116
Hamilton, David, 81

Kunitz, Stanley, 95
Kuspit, Donald B., 18
Kwant, Remigius C., 106

Lahti, A. K., 58
Lakin, M., 63
Lamb, H. W., Jr., 69
Lamb, Howard, 113
Lamb, Hubert, 83
Lamb, Jack Hall, 107
Lamont, Rosette, 113
Landis, Beth McLellan, 83
Langer, Susanne K., 104
Langyel, Peter, 83
Lapham, L. H., 52
Laramee, K. Helena, 18
LaRue, S. M., 4
LaRusso, Dominic A., 107
Leary, Daniel J., 113
Leavitt, Hart Day, 49
Leavy, Stanley A., 95
Lent, John S., 76
Lentricchia, Frank, Jr., 95
Lester, Elenore, 113
Levine, Les, 18
Levine, Paul, 43
Lewis, Allen, 118
Lewis, Clive Staples, 99
Lewis, C., 34
Lewis, G. M., 34
Lewis, Theophilus, 113
Leyburn, Ellen Douglass, 113
Levitt, Theodore, 69
Lichtblau, Charlotte, 18
Lindsay, Sir Harry, 18
Linenthal, Mark, 99
Lippold, Richard, 18
Litsey, D. M., 34
Loehr, Max, 18
Logsdon, G., 18

Lohr, R., 59
London, Sol J., 83
Lorimer, E. S., 4
Lowenfeld, Viktor, 28
Lowes, John Livingston, 100
Lowry, Wilson McNeil, 18
Lubbock, Jules, 18
Lucie-Smith, Edward, 18
Ludel, Susan, 68
Lunacharskii, Anatolii Vasi-
   lievich, 18
Lupton, Mary Jane, 95
Lutyens, David B., 100
Lynch, W. F., 52
Lynton, Norbert, 19
Lyons, John O., 49
Lyons, Joseph, 19

Macchiarola, F. J., 34
MacDonald, D., 52
Machamer, Peter K., 19
Machlin, E., 107
MacInnes, Colin, 19
MacKinnon, Donald W., 19
MacLeish, Archibald, 100
MacLeod, J., 35
MacOwan, Michael, 113
MacShane, F., 95
McCabe, E. A., 4
McCavitt, W., 34
McClerren, B. F., 35
McCluskey, Sister Anne, 83
McCombs, Maxwell E., 70
McCormick, J. E., 57
McCreary, E., 35
McCroskey, James C., 104
McDermid, C. D., 4
McIntyre, John P., 43
McKellar, Peter, 28
McKown, V., 70

McLuhan, Herbert Marshall,
76, 100, 107
McMahan, H. W., 4
McMahan, M., 35
McWhirter, William A., 113
Maier, Norman R. F., 104
Mailer, Norman, 43
Major, Clarence, 100
Malanga, Gerard, 95
Malin, Irving, 49
Malraux, Andre, 29
Mandel, Oscar, 19
Maneloveg, H., 70
Mann, M., 53
Mannes, Marya, 114
Mapes, Glynn, 53
Margolis, Joseph, 19
Margulies, W. P., 4
Maritain, Jacques, 29
Marquis, G. Welton, 90
Marshall, Lenore, 43
Martin, Paulette, 114
Martland, Thomas R., 19
Maslow, Vera, 19
Mathews, Anna, 19
Mathews, Denis, 19
Mathews, Thomas F., 19
Mathieu, Aron M., 49
Matzkin, M. A., 53
Maxwell, M. G., 70
Mayer, Martin, 83
Maynard, H. E., 4
Mazzaro, Jerome, 100
Mee, J. F., 4
Meerloo, Joost Abraham
Maurits, 107
Melville, Robert, 19
Meredith, Robert C., 49
Meredith, William, 20
Merrill, Francis Ellsworth, 20
Merrill, John, 70

Merrill, John C., 70
Messer, Thomas M., 20
Methvin, Eugene H., 70
Metzger, Gustav, 20
Meyer, C., 5
Mial, D. J., 58
Michaelson, L. W., 95
Michelson, Peter, 43
Miller, Arthur, 114
Miller, George, 107
Miller, Joseph J., 100
Miller, Lillian B., 20
Miller, Thomas W., 83
Mills, Jack, 108
Mills, Ralph J., 100
Milner, Marion, 29
Miner, Earl Ray, 20
Mitchell, Donald, 20
Mitchell, Lee, 116
Mitchell, Loften, 119
Moe, E., 58
Mohn, Norman Carroll, 84
Monaghan, Robert R., 58, 104
Montagnon, P., 70
Monts, E. A., 35
Moog, Robert A., 84
Moon, Samuel, 95
Moor, Paul, 84
Moore, E. O., 58
Moore, Harry T., 49
Moraze, Charles, 100
Morgan, Robert E., 84
Morris, Robert K., 43
Morris, Wright, 43
Morse, D. E., 95
Mortellito, Domenico, 20
Morton, Jack Andrew, 63
Moss, J. J., 5
Mothersill, Mary, 20
Moyers, Bill, 70
Mueller, L., 58

Munro, Thomas, 20
Murphy, Francis, 96
Mussoff, Lenore, 114
Myer, John C., 20
Myers, B. J., 35

Nahm, Milton Charles, 29
Nairn, Tom, 21
Natanson, Maurice, 21
Nathan, P., 53
Negri, Numa Clive, 21
Neilson, James, 84
Nelson, G. V., 70
Nelson, L., 35
Nelson, R. C., 5
Nemerov, Howard, 100
Newton, Eric, 21
Nicholson, P. J., 58
Nicoll, Allardyce, 119
Nicovich, George P., 119
Niefeld, Jaye S., 71
Noble, Valerie, 7
Norris, R. C., 35
Norwood, F. W., 35
Novak, G., 5
Novick, Julius, 114

O'Brien, Harold J., 104
O'Brien, Mary Patricia, 100
Ochs, M. B., 5
O'Hara, J. D., 21
Oliver, Robert Tarbell, 107
Olmstead, Donald W., 63, 76
Olson, Elder, 119
Orenstein, Arbie, 84
Osborn, Alexander Faickney, 29
Osborne, Conrad L., 85
Ossman, David, 101
Osterweis, Rollyn, 44

Otto, H. A., 58
Otte, R. W., 35
Oyer, H. J., 35

Pack, R., 71
Pack, Robert, 96
Palmer, E. L., 71
Paltridge, J. G., 71
Parkings, G., 71
Parnes, Sidney J., 71
Patterson, Elizabeth Gregg, 44
Paynter, John, 90
Pearman, Martha, 85
Pearson, Norman Holmes, 96
Peden, William, 49
Pei, Mario, 104
Pelles, Geraldine, 21, 29
Penn, Stanley, 53
Peterson, B. H., 35
Peterson, P. G., 36
Petras, James, 104
Petrullo, Luigi, 63, 76
Pevsner, Nikolaus, 21
Phillips, David, 107
Phillips, Gerald M., 63
Phillips, John, 44
Phillips, William, 44
Piene, Otto, 21
Piore, Quentin, 76
Pirie, Peter J., 85
Plessner, Helmuth, 21
Podhoretz, Norman, 49
Podro, Michael, 21
Polykoff, S., 5
Porter, P., 71
Portnoy, Julius, 21
Potter, Joseph C., 71
Powell, V., 106
Prange, J., 5
Prentice, M., 72

Price, Julia S., 119
Prickett, E., 58
Prideaux, Tom, 114
Pruitt, D. G., 59
Purcell, William L., 85

Rago, Henry, 96
Rago, Louise Elliott, 22
Raines, Charles, 44
Raleigh, Henry P., 6, 22
Ranchoff, Daniel, 22
Raven, B. H., 62
Raven, P., 16
Rawley, P., 36
Ray, H. W., 36
Read, Herbert Edward, 22,
    29, 101
Rees, Garnet, 101
Reimer, Bennett, 85
Remley, F. M., 72
Renan, Sheldon, 54
Reynolds, George Earle, 85
Rhodes, James Melvin, 22
Ricci, Robert, 81
Rice, Elmer L., 119
Rich, Andrea L., 107
Rich, Leslie, 85
Rich, Maria F., 85
Richards, Howard, 22
Richardson, Jack, 114
Richstone, M., 59
Riddel, Joseph N., 96
Rigby, W. H., 36
Riggs, Frank L., 72
Rinn, J. L., 59
Rivers, Isabel, 101
Roberts, George W., 19
Robertson, Bryan, 22
Robertson, F. H., 85
Robertson, R. N., 72

Robinson, J., 96
Rogers, Carl Ransom, 63
Rogers, Harold, 85
Rollman-Branch, Hilda S., 114
Roman, Paul A., 108
Rose, Harold, 72
Rosenberg, Bernard, 22
Rosenberg, Harold, 22
Rosenheim, Edward W., 101
Rosenstone, Robert A., 85
Rosenthal, M. L., 96
Ross, Raymond Samuel, 107
Roth, Nathan, 96
Roth, Philip, 44
Roth, Robert Paul, 23
Rovit, Earl H., 44
Rowland, David, 23
Rowland, H. S., 72
Rowley, P., 72
Ruihley, Glenn Richard, 101
Ruitenbeek, Hendrik Marinus, 49
Rukeyser, Muriel, 96
Rupp, Richard H., 50
Russcol, Herbert, 86
Russell, John, 23
Russell, Paul, 96
Russell, W. M. S., 23
Russo, F., 72
Russo, William, 90

Saal, Hubert, 86
St. Onge, Keith R., 107
Salcedo, Rodolfo N., 107
Salzman, Eric, 86
Samovar, Larry A., 108
Samples, Robert E., 86
Sandberg, Willem Jacob Henri
    Berend, 23
Sander, Ellen, 86
Sandford, William Phillips, 108

Wallace, W. H., 60
Wallen, N. E., 60
Walsh, Chad, 97
Walter, Otis, 108
Walter, Samuel, 90
Warren, Robert Penn, 45
Watson, E. R., 60
Weales, Geraod, 116, 119
Weaver, Andrew Thomas, 105
Weinberg, Helen, 50
Weinstein, Robert V., 88
Weiss, B., 7
Weiss, Margaret R., 25
Weiss, W., 76
Weissman, Philip, 120
Weitzner, Jay, 74
Welden, T. A., 61
Wellworth, George E., 116
Welty, Eudora, 45
Wenkart, Antonia, 26
Werder, Richard Harry, 90
Werner, Alfred, 25
Wersen, Louis G., 88
Wertheimer, Max, 38
Wesling, Donald, 97
West, Rebecca, 45
Wetmore, W. C., 74
White, Gordon, 7
White, H. F., 74
White, Helen L., 105
White, J. F., 74
White, S., 26
Whitney, Edgar A., 26
Whittemore, Reed, 97
Whyte, Lancelot Law, 26
Wiebe, Gerhart David, 25
Wiegand, William, 45
Wieman, Henry N., 105
Wight, A. R., 61
Wilcoxson, I., 89
Wildi, E., 53

Wildman, Eugene, 116
Wilkie, Richard W., 90
Will, Frederick L., 105
Willard, Charlotte, 26
Willett, John, 26
Williams, F. E., 61
Williams, M. G., 37
Williams, Sheldon, 26
Wilson, Colin Henry, 26
Wilson, Frank Avray, 30
Wilson, L. S., 37
Wind, Edgar, 26
Winkler, R., 61
Winthrop, Henry, 26
Wiseman, Molly J., 76
Wiseman, T. Jan, 76
Witty, P. A., 37
Wodehouse, P. G., 116
Wolf, H. R., 61
Wolfe, Tom, 46
Wolfson, B. J., 37
Wollheim, Richard, 26
Wood, R. V., 61
Woods, W. K., 75
Worsnop, Richard L., 75
Wren, G. S., 75
Wright, Charles R., 75
Wurtz, M. H., 89

Yaffe, James, 46
Yamamoto, K., 37, 61
Yeager, Willard Hayes, 108
Yglesias, Jose, 46
Young, Stark, 116

Zander, A., 62
Zaripov, R. K., 89
Zelko, Harold P., 107
Ziller, R. C., 37
Zweig, Paul, 97